Creations in Verse

George C. Clements

Writers Club Press
San Jose New York Lincoln Shanghai

Creations in Verse

All Rights Reserved © 2000 by George C. Clements

No part of this book may be reproduced or transmitted in any form or by any means, graphic, electronic, or mechanical, including photocopying, recording, taping, or by any information storage or retrieval system, without the permission in writing from the publisher.

Published by Writers Club Press
an imprint of iUniverse.com, Inc.

For information address:
iUniverse.com, Inc.
620 North 48th Street
Suite 201
Lincoln, NE 68504-3467
www.iuniverse.com

ISBN: 0-595-00956-5

Printed in the United States of America

*This book is dedicated to the memory of my son,
George Dale Clements, 1948–1976.*

Preface

To dedicate words of what might have a little wisdom is to leave a legacy in writing of pure thought. A legacy to those you love begins the day you are born and grows and develops over the years, through your deeds and inspiration. What we do today will govern the future. Remember that tomorrow, today will be yesterday, and it won't be back. I hope some of the works of this book will fill your heart, and help your mind. In closing, I would like to twist the words of Mark Twain: "My poems are water, those of the great geniuses are wine; everybody drinks water."

A Bird of the Sea

The ocean claims many birds
As part of her domain,
But lets talk of only one,
Maybe later of what remain.
I choose the soaring seagull
As an archetype of grace and charm,
Gliding on the winds that blow,
A creature of peace and calm.
They feed on fish and other foods
That are left upon the shore.
Scavengers maybe, but they are the cleaners
Of what others left before.
Seagulls have no names
And wish to be left in peace sublime,
But they are there for you to gaze on
If you would only take the time.
They symbolize real freedom
As they travel near and far.
They stay close to their ocean,
Not looking for a faraway star.

A Calling from the Sea

I hear a voice calling,
It's coming from the sea.
A beckoning of the ocean,
She says come back to me.

I'm standing on the seashore,
The waves are rolling in.
It's time for another voyage
Where the air is fresh, and another world begins.

Out to the whitecaps
With the mighty ocean swell.
To the domain of the whale,
Or where the flying fishes dwell.

I must return to the sea I love,
To the world of the salty brine.
Out where the sea meets the sky,
Where the two seem to combine.

A Caribbean Experience

I've sailed on the Yankee Clipper
Out through the Caribbean Sea.
From Virgin Gorda
To an isle called Bequia.
I've seen more than a half score of sails
Full with a windward breeze.
I've stood on a heeling deck,
I've experienced all of these.
Climbed the tall ship's rigging,
Supporting three mighty masts.
Had my face washed by the sea,
Both beautiful and vast.
And when we've dropped anchor
Near a shore with a lonely beach,
I've walked barefoot in the sand
With mermaids just out of reach.
No pirate loot or treasure
Ever found by me,
Yet once long ago
This was a pirate sea.
You can still see pirates
Way off on the beam,
If you sleep a good night's sleep,
They're surely in your dream.
If ever there's a place
Where adventure and peace combine,
It has to be on this schooner
And it's friend, the salty brine.

A Caribbean Serendipity

The tropics in the evening,
No words to do it right.
The sky is alive with a thousand stars
Lighting up the night.
A soft moon overhead
Casts shadows on the beach.
The sea comes in rolling swells
From far beyond our reach,
And as they near the shore
They break into gentle waves,
Then recede and try once more.
Palm trees sway slowly,
Sand beneath my feet.
I walk along the edge
Where land and sea compete.
There's a softness in the air
As I take this grandeur in.
Color has changed to deeper tone,
And so the night begins.

A Dad's Legacy

Every dad should leave a legacy
For the children he has sired.
No, it isn't land or money,
It's a man to be admired.
For your children
It begins to build at childhood.
A hero for their lives,
And they will remember when, there, a giant stood.
No you're not a giant,
You're just a common man.
But it's how you handled life,
And your goodness through your span.
What you are and what you've done
Is imbedded in an offspring's mind.
Character and deeds performed,
Are what they would like to find.
So if you leave nothing else
To endear your children's memory,
Leave that strong and kindly giant
In their heart and mind, their library.

A Day So Dear

I have my mementos and memories
Of where I've been and what I've seen.
From the snow cap of Mt. Kilimanjaro
To Ireland, the land of the green.
I've seen the ravages of war
To the people, and what it cost.
Happiness I've found,
Happiness I've lost.
I've flown the clear blue skies,
I've seen the open sea in rage.
I've read so many great books,
And covered every page.
I've had my days of sorrow,
But many more of joy.
I remember years ago,
When just a little boy.
And there's just one thing that is certain,
As elder years appear.
Every day, no matter when,
Is a day to hold so dear.

A Dream or a Vision

Dream a dream,
And if it's good,
Make it live,
Because you know you could.
All great things
Begin with a dream.
You may think it impossible,
Or so it might seem,
But take hold of that vision
And you can make it real.
You know that it's something,
From within you can feel.
The greatest achievements
Man has fulfilled
Was by farsighted people
That went ahead strong willed.
So if you have a dream,
Don't cast it aside.
It might lead to something
That will fill you with pride.

A Dream

To follow a dream,
To trace it down,
To gain a smile,
To lose a frown.
To live a full life
Each and every day
Is why we were put here,
But we must find our own way.
We all have a dream,
But it won't come to us,
It has to be followed,
It doesn't wait as a trust.
Happy the ones
With stars in their eyes.
They know how to travel
To a dream realized.

A Family Prayer

There's coffee brewing in the kitchen.
An aroma to please your taste.
There's biscuits piping hot,
There will be none to go to waste.
Oatmeal bubbling on the stove,
What a way to start the day.
Family sitting around the table,
Time for us to pray.
Each morning someone different
Giving thanks to what's bestowed.
Mom, dad, and children
Reaping what they've sowed.
Each has their day ahead,
They go their different way,
But before the evening meal,
Again they'll stop and pray.
Little things bind a family,
Big things help it grow.
Grace surrounds this gathering,
And love will always flow.

A Fishing Town

Breathe in deep, in this small town,
Down where the ocean be.
Taste the salt in the air,
When the breeze is off the sea.
Fishing boats getting underway,
Heading out to the banks.
Sturdy boats, sturdy crew,
Hard work, danger, little thanks.
But these are fishermen,
And this is a fishing town,
So vessels come and go,
Barometer moving up or down.
And as they return from out on the sea
To the ones they love at home,
The air is full of seagulls
From everywhere they've flown.
There's something very special
In a scene such as this.
The pier loud with anxious birds,
And a town of beautiful bliss.

A Gentle River

The gentle flowing river
Accepted our canoe,
And we moved with the current
Thru a beautiful, quiet world all new.
While the birds sing their songs
And frogs croak and play,
We watch nature's wonders
As we move on our way.
Moss along the shore
And green grass and trees
Whose roots cling desperately
Holding all of these.
The banks that guide
The water gently on its way
Give the turtles
A place to sun and play.
Tranquillity abounds
And peace begins to overwhelm
As nature displays the wonders
Of her ever private realm.
A world of calm serenity,
And we're aloud to share.
All that is asked of us
Is to treat this world with care.

A Giant of a Man

Look at that man
As he walks tall and straight.
Notice his bearing,
His confident gait.
The smile on his lips
Is as sure as the tide.
He has conquered the world
With love at his side.
You call him a man,
But I call him a giant.
To all of his cares,
He is always defiant.
Don't be envious of him
And wish you were he,
But look at yourself,
You're as strong as the sea.
Then with truth in your heart
Examine your soul,
And with God at your side
Set out for your goal.

A Gift

I love the falling snowflakes
That drop from the sky,
The howling wind,
As winter rushes by.

I love the time of year
When flowers poke up from the ground,
And the sun and rain clouds
Take turns and abound.

I love the warmth of summer,
The flowers in full bloom.
Sunshine bakes the earth.
Lightning and thunder make their mighty boom.

I love the time of year
When color takes command.
The air is clean and fresh,
And harvest is in demand.

Take the time to look at snowflakes,
Enjoy the falling rain,
Bask in the sunshine,
And the harvest to sustain.

A Grandfather's Dream

I often wonder
What the world will be
When our great grandchildren
Take the place of you and me.
Will wars have ceased,
And will people be one,
With distrust and hatred gone,
And all bias done?
Will the world be free
For all to enjoy?
Where once again children
May be an innocent girl or boy.
Where hearts reach out,
With a hand to assist,
Wherever it's needed,
And greed doesn't exist.
I hope for my children
That the world will ease as it goes,
To enjoy mother nature,
And smell the rose.
Where no one must be
The first or the best,
Where all over our world,
Only good will is the test.

A Journey

Ponder on an iceberg,
A giant in the sea.
What's hidden below the waterline,
Now that's a lot like you and me.
Wonder where it came from?
How it reached our sight?
Broken from the mother crust
Of a sea of awesome might.
You and I have left a home secure
And ventured out in life,
To begin a new journey,
Have a family, husband and wife.
The iceberg travels with the currents
Into a warmer sea.
Isn't that what we're about
As we venture to what's to be?
But unlike the iceberg,
We're not made to melt away,
We're meant to spread love and happiness
And give it all away.

A Life to Share

To love and be loved
Is a treasure to share,
But it all begins
With a desire to care.
You must give of yourself,
One thing or another.
For the greatest example,
Look to your mother,
Whether you're lucky enough
To have her near,
Or whether she's gone
Without any fear.
Life was made
For those that will love.
Share your life
As planned by our creator above.
If I smile at you
Or hold your hand,
You'll smile back
Because you'll understand
There's someone who
Wants to be there,
When you need a friend
With a life to share.

A Little Advise

A little advise
From someone who knows,
Roses show love
As the story goes.
But if your means
Are shallow and small,
There's a way to give them
And still stand tall.
Twelve red roses
Can be costly dreams,
But let me give you a secret
About what isn't what it seems.
Take a bouquet of daisies
And one single rose in the middle.
You will find out for yourself,
It will solve the riddle.
That one rose will glow
Like the light in her eyes.
You will make her so happy
To your great surprise.

A Little Red Shed

A little red shed
Sets among the trees
Just off the road
Hidden by the leaves.
As I pass it by
On my way somewhere,
I conjure up thoughts
Of why it is there.
Someone sometime constructed this shed
With a purpose of his
And he painted dark red.
It seems unimportant
And that it could be
But there's surely a reason
That it's there by the trees.
I dare not peek in,
For whatever is there
Is private to someone,
As it was built with care.
We all have a private
Little red shed hidden away,
Not always constructed,
Some times in our mind it will stay.

A Little Stone, Maybe Blue

Do you have secrets
Held to you alone?
Moments in your past,
That weigh on you like a stone.
Mistakes are part of life,
None of us may claim perfection.
Carry, if you must a little stone,
A private penance and correction.
You've been forgiven long ago
By everyone but you.
Don't carry what you think a burden,
Just a small reminder, maybe color blue.
It won't take long to feel free,
The blemish will disappear,
And one day you'll hold that stone
And wonder why it's dear.

A Loaf of Bread

My daughter has a breadboard,
She has a rolling pin too.
Mixing flour and water
With yeast and other ingredients, a few.
Next she kneads it all together,
Now it's a ball of dough.
Kneading more and more
Until the consistency is so.
Next comes the bread pan,
Well greased to hold the prize.
While the oven's heating,
She lets it set and rise.
Now into the oven,
To bake just so long,
The air is filled with the aroma,
To the nostrils, it's a song.
And when it's baked just right,
Out of the oven it will come.
To cool before eating,
Anticipation has begun.
You wonder why the rolling pin
Is there but never used.
It's there to protect the precious loaf,
For snitchers will be bruised.

A Man of the Sea

I stand upon the heeling deck,
My hands are on the wheel.
The sky is gray with angry clouds,
The wind is at a gale, I feel.
The jib is furled
And the sails are reefed.
All that's out is a storm sail,
A tiny triangle of some relief.
The ocean is mad at someone,
I hope it isn't me.
I look upon the gray sky
And out upon the sea.
The rain is torrential
As it's pushed on by the wind.
It hits a sailor in the face,
I wonder where I sinned.
What I see before me
Is a reminder of what I know.
That although I am the captain,
The ocean runs the show.
A seagull goes soaring by,
Carried by great wings,
A graceful part of nature's scene,
And the power she sometimes brings.
But there's another side to this ocean
That makes a sailor yearn,
Its a calling from the sea
And so he must return.
A Mermaid

A Mermaid

I'm in love with a mermaid
I met down by the sea.
No one else knows of her,
It's she alone and me.
We would talk for hours
About the world and us.
Many think me off my course,
I can't see the fuss.
Many sailors have a mermaid
They've known a long, long time.
No others ever see them,
That's the same as mine.
A sailor leads a lonely life,
He needs a private love.
With a little imagination,
One is conjured up from the sea or above.
Now what's the harm of a mermaid,
A beautiful girl of the brine,
If she makes a man happy,
Whether she is his or mine?

A Message in Verse

I write what I feel,
I feel what I write.
The words rollout
To kiss not bite.
To put words to form,
And try to please all
Is not the thought,
Just the result of one's call.
Verse and rhyme will make one think,
Whether the story is large or whether it's small
There are those with eloquent words,
And those that ramble away.
There are those that hold words dear,
And those that cast them astray.
But if what's written
Are not words for thought,
Then all the writing
Is to be for naught.
Let serenity reign
While reading verse
And you'll gain something special
As you and the words converse.

A New Day

The day is just beginning
As the sun comes out of the sea,
Cascading a glow of light,
A new day for you and me.
It rises ever so slowly,
A crescent type of glow,
And as I watch mesmerized,
I realize the Lord has made it so.
Right before my eyes,
From a crescent to a sphere.
It's warmth already radiating
From way out there to here.
An aura brightens up the sky
Spreading it's rays of light.
A new day has started,
Replacing the solitude of night.

A Picture Frame

A pitter patter on the roof,
A gurgling at the drain.
Huddled up to the fireplace,
Inside from the rain.
The atmosphere is serene,
There's a crackling in the fire.
A warmth abounds within,
And yet there's a desire.
But for what, I do not know,
As I dream of a time that's past.
I gaze into the glow,
This night will not last.
Moments like this are fleeting,
Then they are gone.
All in life is changing,
And so we too move on.
What is now an instant,
Just becomes the past
All in life is now,
It's not supposed to last.
Another beautiful picture,
In another picture frame.

A Place of Sweet Repose

The air is fresh and clean,
Not a cloud in the sky.
I walk in the sand,
Listen to the seagulls cry.
Gentle waves roll to the shore,
Then slide back to whence they came.
The shore is cleansed and reborn,
Every rock and every sandy grain.
Each small wave or ripple,
Part of nature's scheme of life.
Come to the sea shore,
A respite from one's strife.
Watch the sea, it's waves and swells,
So full of life, in constant motion.
Gulls and terns gliding to and fro,
Eyes ever looking, food be their notion.
Serenity, oh, serenity
You overwhelm all of those
That take the time to gaze and listen
In this place of sweet repose.

A Restless Spirit

There's a restless spirit within me,
To view what I haven't seen.
All around the world,
Sights most couldn't dream.
They start right in our homeland,
And spread around our earth.
Begin with the greatest wonder,
Life's creation, human birth.
Of all the birds and creatures,
I've seen so very few.
Have you ever watched
The forming of morning dew?
From giant mountain ranges
To canyons wide and deep,
That take on awesome colors,
As above the sunbeams creep.
I want to see the redwoods,
Giants reaching for the sky.
The painted deserts of the west,
And hear the eagles cry.
And when I've seen my blessed land,
If time allows it to be,
I'll search the world over
Out there beyond the sea.

A Sailor in New England

Walked down to the boatyard,
It's only March with still a chill.
But something draws a sailor,
Seems he never gets his fill.
Hibernation everywhere,
A place of large cocoons, it seems.
Protection for these precious craft,
And again the sailor dreams.
One more month, be patient.
One more month, be ready,
The wraps will be coming off.
Another winter passing steady.
April is get her ready time,
Refurbish and renew.
May will soon be here,
And again, we'll sail the blue.
The boat bottom is finally wet,
A salt spray washes all
There's still a chill on the water,
But a sailor has heard the call.

A Sailor's Dream

Early in the year, nineteen sixty eight,
There's a fever in the air.
To sail around the world alone,
Who would do or dare?
This voyage would be different,
Although done before.
Nonstop, make no ports of call.
En route, no help to be in store.
If you stop and ponder,
This voyage would take three hundred days
Give or take a month or so,
Depending on the weather and it's ways.
A number of determined sailors
Accepted the chance to try.
Few would ever make it,
But seaward they would ply.
This verse is about the winner,
Robin Knox-Johnston is his name.
His ketch was called "Suhaili",
No voyage made for fame.
Thirty two feet in length,
Eleven feet at the beam,
The smallest boat, attempting
To complete a sailor's dream.

A Single Rose

With long blonde hair
And eyes that sparkle blue,
You smiled and softly spoke
The gentle way I knew.
It warmed my heart,
It seemed unreal,
And yet returned
Soft memories to feel.
You hadn't changed
Your glowing charm,
Becoming more lovely
In your vibrant calm.
A single rose,
Just one today,
Tells all that I
Could ever say.
It holds the dreams
that come with time,
And let's them free
As they join life's rhyme.
Patience holds
My hopes today,
And faith the path
That shows the way.

A Smile

To cause a smile
To replace a frown
To happy laughter
Where there was no sound.
Are you a friend
That can make this be,
And dry the eyes
So one may see?
Life isn't all roses,
The sky is not always blue.
So if the sun isn't shining
For a friend that is true,
Brighten the day
By holding a hand.
Better still, what to do,
A hug would be grand.
Smiles are young,
Frowns make us old.
My friends are precious,
As my life they help mold
Wherever I go,
Whatever I do,
I take a hug and a smile
For someone like you.

A Smiling Face

There are many gifts we can give
In this world, this special place,
And one that is precious
Is a true friend's smiling face.
Just to know there's someone
That cares enough to know
When to share happiness and sorrow
And when to let it go.
That helping hand and heart is there,
It's that sense, you feel secure.
It's a bonding and a kinship
That if nurtured will endure.
But like everything worthwhile,
It must be treated with tender care,
For all of life is fragile,
And worthwhile only if you share.
It's not enough to know someone,
It's not enough for just hello.
It's that caring understanding,
It's something that you know.

A Special Garden

A little rural store
In a little rural town,
Nothing really special,
But it wears a special crown.
It's always filled with comrades
Telling stories of the day.
Some come to spend some time,
And others stop, then on their way.
This store is blessed with flowers
Flowing to and fro.
They're all the girls that work here,
And the girls that come and go.
Your standing in a garden
Where friends come to share
Some very special moments
With people whom they care.

A Special Daughter

You ask for very little,
Yet your heart is full of love.
You're as beautiful as the sunshine
And as graceful as a dove.
You're a woman grown
And a lady fair,
With soft skin, blue eyes,
And long golden hair.
What happened to a time,
Not long ago,
When you were oh so young
And always on the go?
There's a special something
Between daughter and dad,
That causes so much love
That he can become sad.
But the happiness and joy
And the overwhelming pride
Engulfs those sad moments
And casts them aside.
You give to your dad
What no one else may.
You give him a daughter
To love every day.

A Special Place

Majestic ocean,
Mighty sea,
My thoughts keep returning
Back again to thee.
I stand down on the rocky shore
Where there is no sandy beach.
Everything is alive,
From ocean spray to petrels screech.
The waves roll in
And smash against the barrier of stone,
Kicking up an inspiring spray,
Then retreats alone.
But right behind, another crest
Of mighty ocean strength
Comes rolling in again,
To pound this rocky length
That stretches along this coast
As an awesome panorama of beauty and grace.
The forces of nature
Make this a special place.

A Train Called Nostalgia

Just for Nostalgia,
I rode a railroad train.
Headed out of Boston
On a ride down memory lane.
The days of the old steam engine,
For the most part has past.
But memories of those days
Will continue to last.
I remember many years ago,
A two thousand mile ride,
When the train was king,
And it's crew cared for it with pride.
We traveled across our country,
This great land in view.
Everywhere we passed
There was something new.
Small towns and farm lands
Seemed to roll past our sight.
On occasion someone waving,
Much to our delight.
Bridges over rivers,
Prairie land runs for days.
Through valleys and over mountains,
We sped along our way,
Following the railroad track
Over our country, oh, so wide.
Seeing all of this
Has to bring out pride.
A Tribute to a Friend

A Tribute to a Friend

Ralph, you are a special friend
As many will agree,
But there are times ole buddy,
When I'd like to ship you out to sea.
Then you go and turn around
And show what friendship really means.
It's a kinship and caring,
It's the warmth of the Grenadines.
There are those of us who call you
Affectionately "The Bear",
It's a name we chose in humor,
Because we really care.
Now don't get sentimental,
No tear in your eye,
Because you'll lose your image
Of good ole "Captain Bligh".

A View of the Past

We gaze with mighty telescopes
At the heavens all around.
Exploring for something new,
A world not yet found.
Sure enough, there's something there
To excite our curious mind,
But we must realize, because it's so far away,
It's a mind boggling find.
What we see today,
Has just come to our sight.
It long ago may have gone
Even as we view at the speed of light,
We're looking at many thousand years that past.
We see what may not be there,
Oh, once it was, and may be still,
But to know is our challenge and our dare.
The next time you measure mother earth,
As beautiful as she may be,
Remember we are just a speck
In an endless dry open sea.
But be reassured as you meditate,
A greater power made it all.
His plan is for every thing and every place
Whether enormous or very small/

A War of Our World

I would not demean any war,
Or the young that had to die.
I would not demean their loved ones,
Left home to cry.
But let us never forget
The greatest war of time.
World War Two surpassed them all.
It defined your life, it defined mine.
A war where there was no peace,
It covered our land and land a world away.
Yes, it covered our land too,
It taught people how to pray.
There was no nation not involved,
There were no people that it didn't cost.
The world today goes on it's way,
So many not knowing what was almost lost.
We won no easy victory,
We almost lost the war, you know.
Ever think where you might be
If this event were so.
When the Star Spangled Banner
Passes by in a crowd,
Hold your child's hand,
And with the other hand on your heart, be proud.

A Young Man in Love

There's a lovely lass
Dwells in my heart.
She overflows with
The warmth to start
A blaze of love therein
That soon, and even now,
Ignites a conflagration
That must engulf
My heart with
A vibrant love
For this beautiful girl
With the grace of a dove.
A maiden fair
With love sublime,
She is the sunshine
Of the summertime.
Her charm surrounds
Like a rainbow ring.
She is the reason
That a thousand birds sing.
Heaven must have sent
This wonderful girl
Of zeal and zest
To make me whirl.
A lovely lass
Without and within
And blessed with
The name of Marilyn.
Abandoned Dory

Abandoned Dory

An abandoned dory
Lies on the beach.
It's had its day of glory,
Now the sea is out of reach.
Once proud and sturdy,
Now left by itself to rot,
By the kind of person,
Not the seaman sort.
It probably carried and cared for
Many lovers of the sea.
Maybe went with big brother
As it headed out where the whitecaps be.
Could be it was just for fishing,
With solitude only it could give.
Whatever the past,
This sight is sad, as it used to live.
I'm going to restore her,
This nautical part of art.
Yes, that's what it's been
Right from the start.
Very special and sturdy,
With the lines of a seaworthy craft.
Did I say she's a double ender
Proud from bow aft.

Adjust Your Sails

Ponder on this, if you will, for a while.
When a sailor is at sea,
Following his course,
And the wind is not what it should be,
Then he uses his head
And adjusts his sail.
For the wind will change
When it's ready, without fail.
Mother nature is boss,
So if you venture to sea
Plan on accommodating
The powers that be.
Adjust your course,
Adjust your lines too.
Take care of your vessel,
And it will take care of you.
There's one thing more
One should not forget.
It's the Great Fisherman
That casts the net.
Learn to adjust,
Like the petrels that fly.
Keep your hand on the wheel
And your eye on the sky.

Adolescence Missing

I remember when I was a little boy
Three or four feet high.
Everything was fun and games,
I could almost reach the sky.
As time went by and I grew,
The adventures of adolescence
Began to come in view.
Then it happened, " World War Two".
Though young I was, my country, I must serve.
Early I must become a man,
I glorified at my nerve.
So off to a foreign land,
Horror everywhere I went.
Boyhood gone forever,
Into manhood I was sent.
Missing years of adolescence
I can never retrace.
So I go forward with my manhood,
There's still a world to face.

Adventure, Love, and Life

When we're young, adventure looms,
The future is a challenge to be won.
There's very little past,
Everything is yet to come.
Time moves on, we're a little older,
The past is showing up.
And yet for the coming future,
We still hold the overflowing cup.
The years roll on and we mature,
The past becoming wide spread.
But adventure, love, and life are one,
And still a vast unknown ahead.
The secret now is to look beyond,
But never forget the past.
From adventure, love, and life
A solid foundation is cast.
And when we reach a certain time,
And believe most of life has past us by,
Step up and dare the future,
We're a library of knowledge with a world to defy.

Adventure

I took my boat a sailing
On waters with many tales,
Where buccaneers and pirates
Once filled their mighty sails.
The Caribbean Sea
Has many tales to tell,
Where many battles have been won,
And many ships have fell.
Drake was a hero,
They say he served his queen.
Blackbeard was a pirate,
Don't let him near your beam.
There's many more
Great men of the sea,
But for this moment
There is only me.
I conjure up adventure
As a squall comes from the east.
The wind and rain are fierce,
But in a while they'll cease.
That's my adventure,
I don't need pirates
On my beam.
It's a wonderful world we live in
When reality can be a dream.

Advice to the Young

Face into the wind,
Let the rain wash your face.
The sun will shine down
With all of God's grace.
Treat your life like a voyage,
Out on the wild spacious sea,
But never forget your homeport,
And always know where you be.
Know what lies ahead,
Prepare your course with thought,
And before you set sail on your voyage of life,
Know what is about to be sought.
Your vessel of travel is knowledge,
Did you give your teachers a chance
To instill in you a sturdy craft,
Or do you think all of life a romance.
Remember to consider the "Compass Rose"
To keep you on a true course.
Now a "Compass Rose" is a correction guide
On your chart of life from it's source.
Keep faith and be true to yourself,
Then set sail for the stars you see.
And never forget for a moment,
To strive to be all you can be.

Alex's Star

There's a star up in the heavens,
And it twinkles just for you.
It's a billion miles away,
And it's there, very true.
How do you find your star,
The sky seems so full and bright?
You close your eyes and make a wish,
But you must do this at night.
Now open wide, and look right overhead.
There's a very little star,
And it twinkles night and day.
You must remember what it looks like
As it sparkles so far away.
It's only there to see at nighttime,
It's hiding when it's day.
You may give it a name,
And maybe no one else will see.
But all that matters is,
It's there just for Alex, and will always be.

Alicia of the Caribbean

A flower from Jamaica
Came into our lives.
But couldn't stay forever,
You're going home with more learning and very wise.
A single Hibiscus, far away from home,
Filled our lives with an aura grand,
That for many years
Will surround our land.
Alicia of the Caribbean,
Twinkle in your eyes,
The Lord must have sent you
To hearten many lives.
May your days be happy,
Your family will be proud.
Your presence is the sunshine
That chases away the cloud.
Come back to us
On another day.
The best for you and what you do,
Will be heard as we pray.

All of These

No beginning, nor an end,
What is this endless sky?
It's the nothing that holds the everything,
Or our worlds would go awry.
The nothing is our creator,
We look but few can see.
It's one of endless forms,
There's nothing God can't be.
Everything that is about
Is a part of God,
Everything is important,
From endless sky to earthly sod.
A snowflake flutters down,
Another part of Grace.
A flower blooms, then is gone,
Another takes its place.
The rain clouds and thunder,
The babbling brooks and trees,
Yes, and all the birds and we,
The Lord is all of these.

Amanda

Grown to womanhood,
Yes, all too soon.
Her mind in the stars,
Her heart on the moon.
The aurora in the heavens,
No more beautiful than she.
She's found her knight,
As it was meant to be.
She's ready to challenge
The wide world out there,
With this knight at her side,
She offers her life to share.
Leaving Mom and Dad
Is no easy chore,
But she knows her parents
Are still there to love and adore.
There comes a day
In the life of a lovely girl,
When she becomes a woman
And life starts to whirl.
May the sun shine bright
Every day of your life,
With the help of this knight
Who makes you his wife.

An Island of Ice

Way to the north,
Where the ice caps be,
Lies a hidden ocean
Under the ice, a deep green sea.
The world to the north,
Land of glaciers beyond belief.
The ice so thick,
There's little relief.
On occasion, it happens,
A glacier overgrown,
Moves off the land, and out on the sea,
But what the land supports, the sea won't condone.
The ledge breaks off
And floats away on the brine.
Now it's an iceberg,
Majestic beauty, but hard to define.
An island of ice, it has become,
Mostly submerged because it's so dense,
Hard to imagine it's size,
Sometimes immense.
Careful all seamen,
If you venture that way,
And give it some room,
The "ole salts" will say.

Aspirations of a Young Man

Six feet tall,
And I'm a man.
I try to experience
All that I can.
I have my faith,
Work hard, and sports galore.
But that's not enough,
I want for more.
To fulfill my dreams
And all I can be
Takes a wife, then children,
For alone I'm not me.
There's more to a man
Than body and soul,
And without a family
It's an incomplete goal.
Give up some freedoms?
What in return?
Love and attention,
Care and concern.
Sharing all that I am,
And receiving the same.
To marry my love
And give her my name.

Attitude

Age isn't chronological,
It's a matter of attitude,
It's how you're feeling today.
Do you want the world or solitude?
No one is always well,
But there is so many days we're fit.
If you want to stay young,
Learn the joy of fun and wit.
Think with what you know,
Act younger than you feel,
Put a smile on your face,
Face the world with zest and zeal.
Activate your body,
Activate your mind,
And if you have the strength,
Get the two combined.
Disregard what you haven't done,
Take account of what you can do,
Realize you're better off
Than so many you thought you knew.
Once more your attitude is your weapon,
As you fulfill your life.
It's what brings on love and happiness,
And eases pain and strife.

Autumn

Autumn is arriving,
A crispness in the air.
Nature tells the world
With a frost for us to share.
Summer green is leaving, replaced by
Many shades of yellow, orange and red.
Beauty sparkles in the trees,
The colors continue to spread.
Soon we're overwhelmed
With grandeur that comes each year
Sunshine makes all sparkle,
And cloudy days mute the colors that we endear.
There's a special beauty
On the days the sun doesn't shine,
Look a little closer,
This world is yours and mine.
Autumn is a special time;
The end of harvest of what is grown.
A time to reap the bounty
Of what before we have sown.

Awareness Set Free

Take your dog and walk together,
Through the forest just next door.
Throw a stick, she'll return it
And bring it back to you for more.
Listen to the leaves
As the breeze moves them to and fro.
Hear the babbling brook,
Always on the go.
Smell the aroma of the forest
Where the air is fresh and clean.
Let your thoughts meander,
Take the time to dream.
Sit by a sturdy tree
And watch your dog at play
Tension leaves you slowly,
It's now a perfect day.
And when you think you're content,
And your dog lies by your side,
Start to count your blessings,
And slowly you'll regain your pride.

Back Home Again

You can travel the world around
And see its wonders where they lay.
You can share the tropic breeze,
Or see glaciers on their way.
Maybe the jungle of the Amazon,
Or the great Sphinx and Pyramids in the sand.
Maybe the great wall of China
And the temples of the land.
Explore the under ocean,
Or soar into the sky.
You'll find our earth is round
And you'll no longer wonder why.
For whatever path you may choose,
They all return to home.
No matter what you witness,
No matter where you roam.
Exploring our great world,
Is an overwhelming lure,
But when you're done and finished,
It's back to what we call home for sure.

Because of You

The days are filled with skies of blue,
At night the stars shine bright.
You're the reason for the sun itself
As it cascades it's warmth and light.
The waves roll in at the seashore,
Taking turns to greet their queen.
The gulls wing by and sweep in low
To pay respect and display esteem.
You cause the gentle breeze
That freshens on the way.
The hearts of both of us
And makes life bright and gay.
My many thoughts are in need of words
As I gaze into your eyes so true,
But everything is music,
And I'm still in love with you.

Being There

To understand there's someone
That cares enough to know
When to share happiness and sorrow
And when to let it go.
There are many gifts we can give
In this world, this special place,
And one that is precious
Is a true friend's smiling face.
To know that a helping hand and heart is there,
It's that sense of feeling secure.
It's a bonding and a friendship
That if nurtured will endure.
Like everything worthwhile,
It must be treated with tender care,
For all of life is fragile,
But worthwhile if you share.
To share your life in friendship
With others that feel the same
Is a blessing from the Lord
To you who share that flame.

Big Foot

High in the mountain woodlands,
People say a creature lives today.
Some have said they've seen him,
As he wanders on his way.
Tales are told and told again
About his size and hairy frame.
Real or not, he's a legend,
And the world has given him a name.
This lonely sole harms no one,
He stays away from man.
Known only as "Big Foot",
Because of his footprint span.
Suppose he really does exist,
Just as many claim,
Why can't people let him be,
And in his solitude remain?
Yes, it would be nice to know
His lineage and past,
But not by disturbing him
In his home,
The woodlands vast.

Blue Water

The biting spray
Slashes off the sea.
The swells seem like monsters,
They're enough for me.
The wind is howling,
The deck awash a might,
Then scuppered clean
To start again the ceaseless fight
Between my boat and the mighty sea.
But I've got her rigged to do her share,
And we'll come through
Because we paid the ocean's fare.
You say fare, what is that?
It's proven knowledge, you, your boat, and the sea.
Don't venture out on the blue
Until you have all three.
And once you have,
You'll meet a new world.
A ready breeze
With sails unfurled.
A heeling deck
And the wind on your quarter,
Take a deep breath,
There's no place like the blue water.

Books

A row of books on many shelves,
Sitting there by the hour.
A store of knowledge waiting
For you to open and devour.
Take one in your hand and open,
Read, consume, and digest,
This book will take you places
And your mind will do the rest.
You'll learn about the past,
And you'll learn about today.
These are the words of people
Who let their wonder stray.
They came upon the works of life
And put it down in writing.
Every book tells something else.
If you let them, they're all exciting.
The subject matter of a book
Is a choice that you may make.
So read as many as you can
And they will help you to create
A better person than you were
In thought, word an deed.
It's the road to knowledge
And the way to succeed.

Burning Flame

I sit and reminisce,
I think of long ago,
I was a little boy,
Always on the go.
Then I was a teenager,
It follows right behind.
Everything seems like the other day,
That's the way of life in one's mind.
Next I'm fighting someone's war,
Then a marriage is my prize.
Soon children of my own,
It shouldn't be a surprise.
My youth was just yesterday it seems,
Yet today I'm a granddad,
But I'm still that boy,
And you know, I'm, oh, so glad.
I've aches in my joints,
But my attitude is the same.
My yesterdays are still yesterday,
And my heart still has that burning flame.

Changing Seasons

Elusive and fleeting spring,
You seem so far away.
Snow is falling now,
The sky is bleak and gray.

Winter days—so short,
Winter nights—so long.
Bitter winds from the north,
Whistling cold and strong.

Soon the thawing,
The winds begin to ease.
The frost is slowly leaving,
Crocus begin their squeeze.

Up from the soil
Green begins to show.
The sun is warmer,
Blossoms begin to grow.

Spring is in command now,
Taking its place
In the cycle of seasons,
The world is blessed to embrace.

Charlie

Sitting out in front
Of the place that I call home,
Is a friend of mine
Who has no way to roam.
He's a beacon of welcome
To those that come this way.
He needs no food or water,
This sentry here to stay.
No wild call from "Charlie",
He doesn't make a sound.
He stands alert and steadfast,
This seagull so profound.
He's really cast of mortar
And he's handsome to the core.
To me he stands for freedom,
He's the guardian of our shore.
Now Charlie is a strange name
For a friend such as he,
But to me, he's my connection
To the endless, restless sea.

Closing the Rift

What lies deep beneath the sea,
Beyond the eyes of man?
What creatures could exist,
In the depths we've yet to span?
Where unseen mountains hide
And canyons fall away,
Where light is nonexistent,
Another world's hideaway.
We know much about our globe,
Home to all thereon.
Yet we know so little,
How far have we really gone?
There are those that probe for answers
To what we do not know.
Continually, they're learning more,
And with each little more we grow.
The blessing of inquiry
Long has been man's gift,
And surely over time,
Some day we'll close the rift.

Compass Rose

There's a compass rose spread about on every chart
A mariner takes to sea.
It shows a deviation
But the chart doesn't agree.
Longitude and latitude
Make up every chart, it's true.
North is north, and south is south,
But something is askew.
It seems the earth has a magnetic field
That only the compass knows,
And to straighten out this mess,
We have the compass rose.
Each and every one
Is different in it's guide,
As they show the mariner
The true direction of the ride.

Coral Reefs

Coral reefs below the surface
Of any tropical sea.
Living creature that it is,
Look, but let be.
It's grandeur deserves attention,
And the life that dwells about
Depends on it for security,
Always dashing in and out.
Words won't do it justice,
See it just for you.
A beautiful, delicate formation
Continually growing new.
If you have a piece of coral
Broken off by chance,
Keep it with your trophies,
For in there is romance.
To love mother ocean,
Treat her children with care,
For every living thing therein,
This world cannot spare.

Corncob

My dog eats corncobs,
But she would never bite.
All she wants is food and play,
She doesn't know how to fight.
A dog is what you make her,
And mine knows only love.
She never has been angry,
Never push or shove.
She's my constant companion,
Always at my side.
Open the car door,
She wants to go for a ride.
Now she doesn't eat corncobs
As a steady diet,
But she'll eat most anything,
Just give her a chance to try it.

Cotton in the Blue

Puffs of cotton,
Up in the blue.
Clusters of clouds,
Above me and you.
Never the same,
Changing form slowly as we gaze.
Traveling on winds,
To another phase.
What makes the shape
Of what we see?
What makes it happen,
Is it the winds so free?
Endless blue abounds,
Serenity as far as sight,
And hanging there,
The sun shines bright.
Moments of peace,
A place sublime,
And it's given to us.
It's yours and mine.

Dale

There was a man
Who stood strong and tall.
Handsome and gentle,
A fine example for all.
His wealth wasn't money,
Never much of that,
But his smile and manner
Was the throne on which he sat.
He never had a servant,
But friends on every side,
And they walked together
As they had a common pride.
His greatest gift was love and kindness
And he shared it with all.
Until the day came
When the Lord gave him a call.
Too young to go,
But to go he must
And those that loved him
Were left with God's trust.
If you reach the blue heaven
and see a man called Dale,
Call out to him
And give him a hale.

Day Dreaming

Dreaming is a kin to wishing,
It's a little like elsewhere.
It's your own little world
But you're not really there.
Your mind conjures up
A pleasant place or thing,
And suddenly your transported
With whatever thoughts you bring.
It might be a journey
That lasts a little while,
Maybe only a moment,
But either brings back a smile.
There's nothing wrong with dreaming,
It tells of what you are.
It's like holding out your hand,
Reaching for a star.

Daydreaming

My mind begins to wander,
It goes here and there.
The past comes back in memories,
It comes, but from where?
All at once it's yesterday,
Now I'm young once more.
Most things in life are simple,
Never thoughts of what's in store.
Then once again today is back,
Daydreaming is at an end.
Back to what is going on,
It's strange how time can blend.
Next comes tomorrow and beyond,
And what will it be?
The answer is with all of us,
And we'll have to wait and see.
I dream of a future
More like the time of yesteryear,
But tomorrow will be tomorrow,
And memories will remain so dear.

Dilemma

We spend so much time thinking
Of what is going wrong.
Our world seems a dilemma,
But it has for, oh, so long.
We look down,
Yet we should be looking up.
We've been told "it" runneth over,
But we must hold the cup.
We share what is right and wrong
In our lives every day,
But the burden isn't equal,
Some take and some pay.
The dilemma is in our thinking
To straighten out our thought,
For with just a little effort
We can gain the peace we sought.
Try to help someone else,
And see what a difference it makes.
Tolerance and understanding,
The medium of correcting our mistakes.

Do or Don't

To live and do,
To live and don't.
Maybe you will,
Maybe you won't.
But if you do,
Will it be right?
And if you don't,
It's out of sight.
To try and fail
Is no disgrace,
But not to try
Is something to face.
The world is full
Of do's and don'ts.
The world is full
Of will's and won'ts.
A decision to be made,
You can't avoid,
For no decision at all
Is a decision destroyed.

Dreary Day Desires

Cloudy, damp, and overcast,
The air is smite with drops of rain.
Nature seems depressed.
'Oh' to see the sun again
And have serene the starry scope
Of endless blue that spreads above,
To warm the world and reassure
That man holds God's great love.

Dreary day that dulls the heart,
You soon must fade away,
And in your place a better light
Will change the world to gay,
Where once again love may shine
And radiate and flow
To intermingle hearts of those
Who would allow themselves to glow.

Cloudy, damp, and overcast,
This day that is so bleak.
Ole Sol will soon break thru,
With the warmth and cheer we seek.
Look—The rain has ceased
And the clouds are showing blue.
There's the sun up high
Cascading down on me and you.

Ean Chua

I know a girl from Malaysia,
A pearl of the Orient low.
She made her way to America,
And set the land aglow.
Now to succeed in a far off land,
Is no little task to do.
But determined and bright and lovely,
She showed them who is who.
She has a pleasant smile,
And a warmth to pull your heart.
Everyone that meets her
Falls under her spell from the start.
If you're looking for a perfect girl
To fill your heart with love,
Look for a girl named Ean
With the grace and carriage of a dove.

Enchanting Universe

Go out on a calm clear evening
And gaze at any star.
Contemplate its distance
And try to imagine just how far.
Your not looking at today,
But a time long ago.
What you see took place
Before what we think we know.
Imagine if you will,
What is the speed of light,
Just to get an impression of
How far that star is from our sight.
That star is one of millions
With planets orbiting around.
All this is happening,
Yet there isn't a single sound,
In this universe so large
We are a very small part.
Yet we must try to find
Just how it got it's start.
In the meantime look skyward
And be enchanted by the sight,
For God has blessed us
By this sample of his might.

Endless Toil

I dread to think
Of all the things
That I must do today.
The work and toil
Goes on and on,
There is no time for play.
But I will do my very best
As the hours go spinning by
To reach the end
Of all this work,
And when it's done I'll sigh,
And say to me
I'm glad I could
Do all the things
I know I should.

Endless

Our world is part of many worlds
From the heavens far away,
To creatures so minutely small
We wont see them in our day.
With all the tools we work with,
They can only search so far.
The smaller worlds are as distant
As the farthest shining star
We are part of endless time,
A small part to be sure,
We've been blessed with intelligence
So we know we're insecure
All the knowledge we think we have
Wouldn't show up on the larger scene.
There are worlds out there, small and large
That doesn't know we're a part of the scheme.
Yet knowing this we continue to believe
We're going to save it all,
With discord among each other,
Not listening to the call.
Our Great Creator gave us what we have
And we continue to call for more.
We must have faith to believe
That we will enter God's great door.
If a person wants to
He or she can start

By showing endless gratitude
And action from the heart.
The Lord has shown his love
And now it's up to you.
Your day of redemption
Is long overdue.

Eons of Knowledge

There's so much to learn,
So much to teach.
Endless eons of knowledge,
And all within reach.
Take a book in your hand
And read what has passed,
Apply it to today,
And part of tomorrow you cast.
All that there is
And all that will be,
Began with learning
In a time before you and me.
We're not the beginning,
Nor are we the end,
Our mission is to continue to learn,
And take that knowledge and send
It to those that follow
With an inquisitive mind.
They will teach others
Of the treasures we leave behind.
Knowledge is second only to love
In the salvation of man,
For they control health and inspiration
In all of life's span.

Erin

Sparkling eyes
And raven hair,
A heart of love,
And a soul of care.
I know this girl
That radiates a glow
Of sunshine and flowers.
The Lord made her so.
She casts a spell
On all that is near
And captivates the lucky ones
That can say they hold her dear.
One lucky man
Won this prize,
And now he's hers
To his surprise.
He chased her till she caught him.
Two beautiful children, their reward.
Because this ray of sunshine
Was sent to us by the Lord.

Faith in Life

A heart is heavy
And dreams are blue.
It happens when
All the things we knew
Begin to run
Beyond our reach.
As the sea recedes
And leaves the beach.
What do we need
To bring back the tide
Where a man walks tall
With all his pride?
As the tree stands high
In all its splendor,
Think of the uses
It's there to render.
Be like that tree
And spread out your beauty.
Life is God's gift,
To live it your duty.
You have faith in the tide,
You know it returns.
Have faith in this life
As long as love burns.

Faith

I wonder where, I wonder when,
I wonder how, I wonder why.
Man is born and lives his life,
He grows old, his time to die.
What is life, where is it from?
He passes on, to where we do not know.
There's a light at either end,
Something makes it so.
Words passed down
From ancestors past.
Signs are seen by a chosen few,
Then passed on, a legend cast.
A need to know
All is well,
A belief is born,
In our mind, it will dwell.
Interpretation of a word,
The wonder of a sign,
The reason for deviation
Of thoughts that don't align.
To those secure,
They've gained a faith to tower
Above uncertainty and fear.
They know the hands of a higher power.

Family

The greatest gift given to you
From the Lord up above,
Next to life itself,
Is a family to love.
Your friends are a special gem,
To be treated with love and pride,
But your family is a part of you
And always at your side.
The world can be a lonely place
To those that know no kin.
Your family pours out its love,
But you must let it in.
Your family is your wealth,
No matter what else you may think,
They are your reservoir of strength,
From which you may always drink.
As for me, I am grateful
For the gift of those I call mine.
They bring forth the stars at night,
In the day, the sun to shine.

Feelings in the Fog

There's a foghorn on the point,
But it can't be seen by me.
I'm standing on the shore
Where the land meets the sea.
The beacon of the lighthouse
Barely sheds a glow.
The fog is dense and heavy,
The ocean calm as ripples come and go.
Everything is quiet but the foghorn,
The sea seems at rest.
Now and then a seagull breaks the silence,
A time of reflection, when thinking is at it's best
No need to be a seaman
To enjoy this lonely place,
Where you're alone with nature
And the world has slowed its pace.
What I am comes forward,
And I face myself to know,
Whether I live my life,
Or simply let it flow.
I refuse to do the latter,
For I must be me,
And do and think my way,
That's the only way to be.

First Break of Light

If you live in a place
Down close to the shore,
You have a picture
Of beauty galore.
Rise in the morning
At the first break of light
And turn to the east
To a wondrous sight.
That great ball of fire
Where the sea meets the dawn,
Will inspire your heart
And make your life spawn
Into what could be
The beginning for you,
The greatest of moments
In your life thru.
To be inspired by love
And by nature as well,
Is all that it takes
For man to excel.
So when you are filled
With that radiant glow,
Go out in the world
And make yourself grow.

Fountain of Youth

The fountain of youth
Is in ones mind.
To be young at heart
And wise combined,
To form an attitude
Of what you are,
To be content to know
Your not a star.
For life as we know it
Is more than it seems.
A babbling brook
Can be a river of love.
A bird overhead,
A gracious dove.

Free as the Breeze

A sandy beach,
A blue coral sea.
A blazing sun,
They belong to me.
A gentle breeze,
My sloop nearby.
The breeze picks up,
Sand in my eye.
We can't have that,
My boat is crying.
Get aboard, we've got a breeze,
Time for sailing, no denying.
Pull in the hook, raise a sail,
Yes, we're moving, we're under way.
Gear stored, all sails set,
Wind in my face, an ocean spray.
I don't set a course,
I don't keep a log.
A squall's okay,
Very seldom fog.
I'm the captain, I'm the crew,
I'm as free as the breeze.
So come along,
And share all of these.

Friendship

Make a friend of someone,
It will come back to you,
For friendship is the greatest gift
That you can ever construe.
Don't look for some return,
Because you've given such a gift.
Friendship is a sharing
That gives both your lives a lift.
Remember, it's not a certainty
That never needs some care.
It's an ever growing bonding
For lucky ones to share.
Give a great big smile
When you approach anyone at all,
You never know, it could be
The start of another friendship call.
There are many people in the world
Either lonely or very shy,
So never hesitate
To raise their spirits high.

Friends

To laugh and jest,
To hope and try,
And be at rest
And chase the sky.
If you want and if you will,
Join with me
And your life I'll fill
With all the joy
That I can claim.
Just be my friend,
All I ask is you remain.
When two worlds mingle as one
And someone cares
There's twice the fun.
To laugh and jest
Through sun and rain,
And when it's done
Two friends remain.
We make our joy,
It not a gift.
Share yourself with others
And give the world a lift.

From Me to You

I write what I think,
And I think what I write.
It's an effort by me
To shine some light
On those that I love,
And those that care
To sit and read rhyme
That I try to share.
Stories to tell,
Some tall, some short,
That give me pleasure,
And give me pride.
Verse is written from within,
It comes and goes much like the tide.
Few please all
And all may please few,
But I must please me,
And every line is written anew.
As you read the words,
Keep one thing in mind,
It's written with hope
That enjoyment you'll find.

Frontiers

Frontiers are neither north or south,
Nor are they up or down.
They're where man's mind takes him,
They're where he finds renown.
Think of what might or could be,
Then try to make it so.
Imagine, if you will,
A place where only you will go,
Exploring with your mind
A vision that is yours.
Dream of things that never were,
Then make them your private cause.
Everything except our world and universe
Has come from someone's mind,
For they looked for an answer
And created one more find.
The limit of what's to be
Has yet to come in sight,
For as long as man has vision,
There's no limit to the light.

Generations

My pride is not in me,
But in the ones I've sired.
Children, grandchildren, great grandchildren,
I only hope I've inspired.
If you stop and think
Your family is you, mighty and strong,
And as long as they venture forth,
You're going right along.
To give your family
All the love you've got
Is to give them
Much more than they ever sort.
You think you love,
And probably do,
Believe it or not,
More comes back to you.
If there's ever a time
To show how you care,
Right now is the moment
With whatever you dare.
Of the moment we speak,
It's already gone past,
Only what you do now,
Can you make last.

Give It Away

Yesterday is a memory,
Tomorrow is a dream,
What we do with today
Governs both it would seem.

Memories are bad and good,
No one will deny,
So put on a cheery face
And a twinkle in your eye.

Make today for someone
By giving them an embrace,
Everyone is wanting,
You'll see it in their face.

And your reward you wonder,
What could it be?
Maybe sharing love,
Will bring some back to thee.

A friend is a wonder,
A richness beyond compare,
And all you have to do
Is give warm and friendly care.

Love is a part of you,
But it isn't there to stay.
It's you in your glory
That you must give away.

Give Me All of These

Give me the spray
Of an ocean wave
As the bow of the ship
Dips into the sea.
Give me the bite
Of an ocean breeze.
Let me feel the heeling deck.
Give me all of these.

Let me hear the cry of ocean birds
As they soar above the waves.
Let me race with Dolphins,
And watch flying fish play.
Let me sight the mighty whale
Give me all of these , if I may.

Let me experience tranquillity.
Yes, and let me fight a gale.
And when it's time
To bid farewell to the sea,
Let me rest and tell my tale.
Give me all of these.

God Is Speaking

Can you hear God speaking?
He's talking to you now.
If you don't it's because you're not listening
Or you don't understand how.
The whisper of the wind,
The rustle of the breeze blown leaves,
The patter of the rain,
His voice is all of these.
The smile of a stranger,
The sunshine in the morn,
It's the twinkle of the stars above
As another babe is born.
The Lord's language is simplicity,
Not made of nouns and verbs.
It's in the blooming of a rose,
It's in the growing of the herbs.
His words are in this beauty,
Seen only by the wise.
It's what we take the time to view,
And what we will recognize.
Our Creator gave us everything,
We need not ask for more.
Give him thanks for what we have,
Give him thanks for what's in store.

God's Plan

To learn one must experience,
To profit one must spend,
To receive one must give,
To live one must defend.
We only learn by doing,
But doing takes some time.
The time we give reaps knowledge,
With knowledge we learn of nature's rhyme.
There is no peace if we don't accept
The world of another's thought.
We spend too much time denying
The beliefs of what others sought.
Whether everyone agrees or not,
The Great Creator is the same
No matter where you roam,
He may be known by a different name.
Perception is what is different,
As history has spread its wings,
Stories told are stories changed.
That's the way of things.
Don't waste your time on what seems disbelief,
For variations are part of God's plan,
From each and every mind and soul,
From each and every kind of man.

God's Children

Don't try to be something or someone
That you're really not,
Just be yourself and you will gain
All the things you've sought.
Life is very real,
It isn't make believe,
And when you bend the truth
It's only you that you deceive.
Each and every person
Has a private gift to give,
And they can only give it
If it's from the life they live.
Yes, some are born to an easy time
And some from destitution.
Some cross over that
Because of resolution.
Then there are the ones in between,
Who struggle every day just to keep in stride.
But whatever group you're bound to,
You can live your life with pride.
You're one of God's children,
Very special in every way.
You are not forgotten,
He's with you every day.

Harvest in the Spring

Like acres of flowers in bloom,
The hills have turned to colors to astound.
At nature's bidding, they become muted.
Then the pilgrimage, they fall to the ground.
Where color now turns to brown,
And each year decompose for the season ahead,
To enrich the soil.
Mixed with snow and rain, it's fed.
Temperatures lower, weather becomes wild.
Winter is upon us, the beauty of white.
But she can be harsh
When she shows her might.
But if we wish to enjoy
The blooming of spring,
The earth must be nurtured
By the dormant freeze winter will bring.
Life abounds beneath the frozen soil,
And winter only slows
Nature in it's toil.
There's a harvest in springtime,
If you stop to think.
The ground thaws and pops
Blue, red, yellow and pink.

He Stole My Daughter

Listen to a story of a man gone good.
Tom, Tom, that son of a gun.
He stole my daughter
And away he run.
But the one thing he could not take,
I was her first boy friend,
And that he will never shake.
When it comes to men,
He's at the top of my list
Of the things a father
Should always insist.
To know this man
And to agree and understand
May not always happen,
But our friendship is beyond grand.
He loves my daughter,
And grandchildren too.
Put that with his dedication,
And that's how our love grew.
I wouldn't swap that man
For all the tea in China,
Because I believe
They don't come any finer.

Highway Show

I'm sitting by the highway,
The traffic speeding by.
Fast, much too fast,
They're in a rush, but why.
Out of the way, they're screaming,
I've got to go somewhere.
Horns are blowing, make way.
Stress in every driver, they don't seem to care.
Now and then an accident,
Lets hope no one paid the price.
Why won't they slow down,
And take a little advice.
Behind the wheel you're the master,
How little you really know.
One little error by anyone,
And that ends your highway show.

Hope for the New Millennium

Time rolls on and on,
A thousand years have past.
A thousand things we've learned.
Now a new millennium is cast.
We've learned we're not the center
Of all the stars that surround,
But merely a small planet
Circling our sun, round and round.
In an instant we can see around the world,
Or even outer space.
But we've yet to learn
There's more than one path to our Creator's Grace.
Will we learn when the universe began?
Did God create the great outward blast
That carries on today?
How long will it last?
Where did it all begin?
Has anyone been told?
Everyone must keep their faith.
This may be the millennium for the truth to unfold
Ever since creatures walked.
They battle in the name of the Lord, yes it's yet to cease.
Maybe in the new millennium,
All will learn to live in peace.

House Guest

I've got a friend in my house,
Not an unwanted guest.
A gentle little creature
Who at night time shines his best.
My friend is a cricket,
And although I love his sound,
I would like to find him
And put him outside on the ground.
He surely must be lonesome,
And maybe hungry too.
So I'm in a dilemma,
I don't know what to do.
He has a friendly call,
And I'm sure his life's askew.
But I can't seem to find him,
His beep-beep, his only clew.
What do you feed a cricket,
Does he need a drink?
You wonder why I worry,
Well just stop and think.
He's a living creature
With the right to life as you,
So he should be cared for,
That's not much for us to do.

I Wonder

I look up to the heavens,
I choose a single star.
Oh, so far beyond our reach,
How big, where, how far?
I wonder how, I wonder why,
Filled with stars,
This wondrous sky.
I wonder if the star I chose
Still is shining bright,
As it was long ago
Cascading on us tonight.
For as I gaze on this panorama,
I'm looking at the past
And I have to wonder,
How long all this can last?
This spectrum puts things in perspective
As I gaze behind our time.
It makes one wonder if in a million years
Someone else will see our star shine.

In a Flash

There's one thing sure in nature,
That nothing remains the same
Neither you or I, or the clear blue sky;
We all are part of the game.
The sand on the beach,
Or the clouds in the sky;
The stars in the heavens
As they streak by
We age by the moment
And a new person appears.
So does all things in nature,
In the flash of a moment, not in years.
Be what we are
And give it our best,
Old mother nature
Will take care of the rest.
Every moment we spend
Is gone so fast.
We cannot repeat it
Nor can we make it last.
What should we do
If we think this way?
Live good every moment,
Live good every day.
But in order to do that
As we change so fast
Is to send love to others
And be sure that it lasts.

In The Lord I Put My Trust

When the sun is shining bright,
And the sky is clear blue,
When there is a gentle breeze,
My thoughts go back to you.

When the rain comes down in torrents
And the sky is full of lightning,
When the thunder booms shake the sky,
My thoughts go back to you.

In the quiet of the evening
As I lie alone in the dark,
I think of all the joy we had,
My thoughts go back to you.

I wake in the morning,
A new day is beginning.
I get that lonely feeling,
My thoughts go back to you.

My life is in my hands, I know,
I do what I must.
My thoughts go back to you,
But in the Lord, I put my trust.

Inner Feelings

I torture myself in private thought,
Deep distress tears me apart.
Lonely within, lonely without,
What do I do, Where do I start?
My mind is in a turmoil,
It's straining to call.
But to call for what,
I'm not sure at all.
Not a single picture,
Many just as me.
So few to listen,
So few to want to see.

Inner Peace and Outer Peace

Peace, oh peace, evasive peace,
The world won't let you be.
Yet every soul there ever was,
It's you they would like to see.
There's a secret to be engulfed by you,
Yet man knows it not.
Ever since there were only two,
He and she have fought.
A waste, a waste, to disagree
To the point of causing strife,
We've all been put together
To enhance each other's life.
We have so much,
We see it not.
All of time we spend at war,
And ignore the peace we've sought.
The inner peace, the outer peace,
They will be found some day.
The lack of one is self-confined,
The other leads the world astray.
It doesn't have to be
If we take each other's hand,
And listen to the heart,
And try to understand.

Inspiration

The sun rose bright in the east
To begin a brand-new day.
The sky is a brilliant blue
In the heavens far away.
My thoughts turn to joyous things,
The world seems so right.
That's called inspiration,
Carried by days first light.

Now the sun is setting in the west,
Slowly sinking low beneath my sight.
The sky now full of shades of color
From reds to blues and grays, everything is right.
The sun now is gone,
The stars put on their show,
Sparkling in the heavens,
All above is aglow.
That too is inspiration
Caused this time by fading light.
Everything is tranquil,
All seems so right.

Then there's the ocean,
The waves come rolling in.
Cascading over one another,

Who knows where they begin.
If you watch and listen,
Your cares begin to go.
This is mother nature
With another inspiration show.

It's Home for Me

I use to dream and travel
To lands so far away,
To visit world wonders,
See strange people at work and play.
But as I've become older,
I see the joys of home,
And the drive to travel dims.
I lose the urge to roam.
People travel all the world
To see what is far away,
But their greatest moment
Is returning home to stay.
I've seen exotic places,
Wild animals roaming free.
I've seen majestic mountains,
But it's here at home for me.

Give It Away

Yesterday is a memory,
Tomorrow is a dream,
What we do with today
Governs both it would seem.

Memories are bad and good,
No one will deny,
So put on a cheery face
And a twinkle in your eye.

Make today for someone
By giving them an embrace,
Everyone is wanting,
You'll see it in their face.

And your reward you wonder,
What could it be?
Maybe sharing love,
Will bring some back to thee.

A friend is a wonder,
A richness beyond compare,
And all you have to do
Is give warm and friendly care.

Love is a part of you,
But it isn't there to stay.
It's you in your glory
That you must give away.

Jessie

Jessie, oh Jessie
You've left us behind
To journey with God,
And for that we don't mind.
Your parents are waiting,
Mary, Beth, and Louis too.
You've blessed this world for near ninety nine years
With love and kindness and what you would do.
Your sister, children, and friends
Will someday join you above,
But, for now, there's no way of filling the void
That you left with all of that love.
Now Jessie, there is something
That all think they should know,
and it's very important you see.
Your apple pies, where did they go?

Judgement

The world today
Seems critic or grace,
Black is black, white is white,
No room for gray when we should erase.
We make a judgement,
Right or wrong,
And expect the world
To go along.
But who are we
To cast the shame,
Whether a person is innocent
Or whether to blame.
When judgement comes
From those who know,
Lets wait for them,
For the truth to flow.
Some lives are ruined
Because the past seems black
Yet many of these
Were given no slack.
Some lives are glorified,
Their past seems pure white.
We know not their inner selves,
That too could be a sight.
All of us have secrets
That we want to keep secure,
The world won't let us do it,
We are either bad or we are pure.
Nothing is perfect,

Whether human or not.
It's a goal to be set,
It's a goal to be sort.

Knowledge Without Peace

How far the world has come
This last one hundred years,
The things mankind has learned
Has brought us hope, joy, and fears.
We have found so many ways
To better health and life.
We talk around the world,
But it hasn't improved the strife.
It's time to slow life down,
And think of the other guy.
Is it possible for one on one,
To bring the peace that comes from on high?
Or is there such a thing,
An elusive peace to find?
Man and animal alike,
Have always fought with kind.
I can not change the world alone,
But if I can think of you, and you can think of me,
We can spread love and hope
And maybe others will see.
Yes, these words are dreams,
But that's what motivates our thoughts,
To accomplish what is gained,
A simple smile and embrace must be sought.

Leaving the Ground

I'm sitting in the cockpit
Of a giant jumbo jet.
We're ready at the runway end,
But it's not our turn yet.
Now the tower says it's clear to go,
So we throttle up the jet.
We start to move into place,
Then quickly pick up speed.
Soon the instrument panel tells us
We have the speed we need,
So we pull back on the yoke
And begin to lift aloft.
It's such a wonder feeling
As we leave the ground so soft.
Now we're gaining altitude,
Soon breaking in the blue.
Once again we check the panel
And we're on our way anew.

Lee

It was time to go,
She was ninety three.
So in her dory,
She headed to sea.
Her Creator was calling
From the height of the crest.
She had given her all,
It was time for her rest.
The vacuum she left
Is filled with memories and love.
Look to the heavens,
For the new star above.
Farewell Lee,
Mother to all.
Her legacy is memories,
As she answers the call.

Legacy

Look ye people who appreciate beauty,
At that Grandfather clock, standing there.
An artwork so noble and proud.
Constructed with hands of loving care,
It ticks away as minutes fly,
But on the hour it becomes loud and true.
A clear beautiful chime then rings out
And sings the time to me and you.
Now watch the pendulum
As it moves to and fro.
Be mesmerized for a moment
And feel your anxieties go.
It's made of pure mahogany from a land far away,
And delivered to the craftsman,
Who forms it another day.
Peruse what is sculpture;
Don't miss a single curve.
Because what you see is gentleness,
Almost living, standing but to serve.
Now give a thought if you will,
To the craftsman no longer there.
He has left a valued legacy
Through his loving care.

Life Rolls On

I find myself
In rhyme and verse,
All is forward,
There's no reverse.
Life rolls on
And so must we.
To reminisce of days gone by
May guide us to what's to be.
Dream you will of what's in store,
For there's creation there for you to design,
And by it's very nature,
You'll improve and refine.
How to begin, how to do?
With a gentle heart, and a caring soul,
And a love to learn
These the secret of your goal.

Life's Fare

Life moves towards tomorrow,
Yesterday is now behind.
The present is just an instant,
Then a memory in our mind.
Make each moment special
That you're proud to hold and claim,
You may remember it tomorrow,
By then it's in your fame.
The world will be a better place
With whatever good you do.
When tomorrow is today,
It's all because of you.
You listened to the singing birds,
Took time to smell the flowers.
You were mesmerized by the sunrise and sunset,
And you walked in the showers.
Now that doesn't sound like much,
But you radiated warmth and peace,
And it will flow forever
And never will it cease.
No one will probably notice,
Maybe no one will care,
But you've made a contribution
And that's life's only fare.

Listen and Hear

Some won't agree
To what I say,
But a while ago
I learned to pray.
If you speak with God,
Be prepared to hear,
For it's a conversation
And demands your ear.
It's proper for one
To give thanks and ask,
And if you give it some thought,
It won't be a task.
Listen to God
As you're spoken to.
You say you can't hear him,
Well, that isn't true.
The breeze in your face,
The rustle of leaves,
The rain on the window,
He is all of these.
The tide rolling in,
The bird with a call,
The lord is speaking
Through one and all.

Listen to the Writing

As I sit with and read
A book of verse,
I hear the words of an inner voice
As their creator and I converse.
Poets let free to flow
Their thoughts, hopes, and dreams.
They are saying in words so soft
What is in their heart it seems.
Listen to their work of words,
If you will, and by doing such
You answer to their voice,
Their yearning to be heard so much.
There are thoughts in every line,
It matters not nature, woe, or cheer,
They are creating in word, emotions
For you and me to hear.

Listening to a Verse

A pen writes a picture,
It draws it in your mind.
Everything is color,
It's there for you to find.
Listen to the words
The scribe writes for you,
For only in verse
Will you get a proper view.
Verse is words of feeling,
The opening of a soul,
And what flows out
Simply seems to roll.
Smooth and gentle sometimes,
Smashing, crashing on another day.
But the way of verse conveys a message,
For it has thoughts to say.
There's sedation in composing,
It's a gentleness within.
It's a way of offering something,
To those who will listen in.

Living Life

What are you doing,
Act your age, I've been told.
But what is my age,
It's what my mind does hold.
You can be young at heart and spirit,
If your life can be a joy,
But only if you take hold of it,
You're not a little girl or boy.
There are many days
You're not your best,
That's part of growing older,
Now—What do you do with the rest?
Enjoy every moment
On the days you're feeling good.
Never mind the opinions
Of what others think you should.
We're all on a one way road,
You can make it tranquil or serene,
You can make it full of zest,
But carry out your dream.

Love Makes a Home

What makes a home a home,
Very simply defined.
It's not shelter, warmth, and comfort.
It's the intertwining love combined.
To have and hold,
Not golden rings and bands,
But a gentle hug or kiss,
Or even holding hands.
This is where the shelter is felt,
Where the warmth gracefully begins.
To know you're not alone—the comfort,
And everyone surely wins.
The sun will add its brightness,
The moon will cast a glow.
The home will radiate because
Love is in a constant flow.

Love of the Sea

The love of the sea
Is nothing that's taught.
It's something within you,
That need not be sought.
The air at sea,
With it's salty taste,
Wraps around you
As nature's embrace.
Whether the sea is calm,
Or a gale may blow,
A sailor is free,
And the sea made it so.
You look up at the sails,
There full with the breeze,
And you thank the Lord,
He gave you all of these.
Serendipity, the gift
Of those who chose
The unpredictable ocean,
A place of repose.
As you read these lines,
Remember the gift of life that be
Is dependent on
The great vast sea.

Love, All There Is

Three score and ten,
And yet I sit and yen
For what, I do not know.
Yet I want it so.
Will I ever be content
With the wonders God has sent?
Why this constant pull
To make my life so full,
When all there is, is mine,
And yet I can't define
All the joys I hold within.
Yet I know I should begin
To understand and realize
That maybe I'm now wise.
And if I listen to my heart,
My yearnings will depart,
Remembering my special lift,
My children's love, no greater gift.
When spirits descend and are low,
It's my loving family, that brilliant glow.

Love

A rose grows in a garden,
This one is a brilliant red.
A boy gives it to his girl,
Words need not me said.
When did a rose become a symbol
Of affection and of love?
No one knows the answer
But the good Lord up above.
A rose needs care to make it last,
Love is just the same.
It must be always nurtured,
As a fire needs a flame.
Its expression changes over time.
It becomes much more serene,
And if your very careful
It will become an everlasting dream.
Cherish your good fortune.
Cherish the one you love.
It will come back to you,
That's from the Lord above.

Lovely Ladies on Easter Day

Ladies in dresses
New and bright,
With pretty bonnets
On their tresses delight
The hearts of those
Who may
See them as they
Parade on Easter day.

Happy and beaming, their faces
Show how proud
The ladies are
In the crowd
Of people who
Must agree and say,
How lovely the ladies
On Easter day.

All are young
In spirit and dress,
And as they go by
We must confess.
It's the ladies
That make so gay,
Each and every
Wonderful Easter day.

Made for You and Me

Bright blue skies,
Cotton floating free,
This spring day
Was made for you and me.
Oh spring, I see you in the morning sun,
I smell you in the air,
I feel you in the blowing breeze,
This day that is so fair.
Crocus up and blooming,
Narcissus, then tulips just ahead.
Warm thoughts of love,
A time the soul's re-fed.
The breeze, so refreshing,
Spring rains come then go.
And then the sun is back,
Everything's aglow.
Magic is this time
That turns hearts to love.
A bird flies by overhead,
A robin, no, this time a dove.

Madison

To sit and write a verse or two
About a little girl so dear.
To say the things that should be said,
I try to write these lines so clear.
If your children are the love of your life,
What are the words for those they bare?
Another generation born of love,
Grandchildren for pride and loving care.
Next comes what we didn't see
As the grandchildren have grown up.
Another generation born,
The Lord has surely filled our cup.
Great grandchildren come into our world,
To most it's only a dream.
But to those of us that are so blessed,
It's more than it would seem.
To have another child to love,
This special gift is mine.
A little girl called Madison,
A gift from the Great Divine.
Mom and dad are, oh, so proud,
Grandmother and granddad too.
But you can't begin to realize,
What great grandparents think of you.

Make Your Own Decision

Are you sure of what your doing
Is the question of the day.
Everyone has their opinion
And all know what to say.
But maybe just for once
If you really try,
You can make up your own mind
And bid advise goodbye.
Everyone means well,
We want to help each other.
It's very hard to offer silence
When the answer we discover.
The problem of today
Probably will be tomorrow past,
But even if it isn't
The answer will come at last.
Whether we are giving,
Or whether we receive,
Advise is well meaning
And we only want to please.
Friendship is a wondrous thing,
It's a meeting of the heart.
It's there at the end
As it was at the start.

Mankind's Belief

The Bible has much to say,
We all listen in a different way.
What you read is what you see.
What I read, a difference be.

One Lord, many a name,
Each of us right, there all the same.
Who are we to say it's wrong
If someone else doesn't go along?

Interpretation of every line,
It will differ, yours and mine.
Read the Bible and believe,
Draw on the faith you retrieve.

Faith is a private blessing,
Not a thing of prepossessing.
God did not put us here
To judge the faith of our peer.

Grant the right of every soul
To understand the good Lord's goal.
Believe how you will, let others the same.
Because you disagree, do not defame.

Manneken-Pis

A little boy in Belgium
Many years ago,
Became lost from his parents.
He wandered to and fro.
Now his father was a rich bourgeois
With influence galore.
He offered a reward,
Then he offered more.
To build a statue of his son
On the very place he was found,
Doing what his son was doing,
He'd buy the very ground.
Now legends say the boy was sighted
Standing on the corner performing great relief.
He saw nothing wrong with that,
He was only a little boy and could see no grief.
True to the word of his father,
A statue was conceived
In the form of a fountain,
Where his son was relieved.
If you should ever visit Brussels,
The statue of the boy is there.
An unending stream is flowing,
The little boy is bare.
Before you judge this story
And think it might be this,
Ask anyone in Brussels
Where is the Manneken-Pis?

Marriage Is Like a Flower

A seed is planted,
It begins to grow.
If it's nurtured
A bud will show.
A blossom blooms
With tender care,
A thing of beauty,
All too rare.
A marriage is a planted seed,
And it takes two to make it grow.
But with love and tender care,
You will reap all you sow.

The Massai and Neighbors

There's a strong and proud people
That live among the wild.
There neighbors are the wildebeest,
The zebras and gazelle are mild.
They have many other neighbors
But they don't seem to fret.
There are monkeys, leopards, and elephants,
and giraffes, lest we forget.
On occasion there's a rhino
Or even a hippo too.
There are many beautiful birds,
And for all the watering holes are few.
They also have the lions
And they deal with them each day.
For they are the troublesome
In this land that's full of prey.
Back to the people
That live their lives with care.
They will fight for their possessions
And the lion best beware.
For if they lose a cow
To a lion on the hunt,
They will track down this great cat
And avenge the wild stunt.
These people are the "Massai",
They live as a family team.
If by chance, you meet them,
They are courageous people and rate your esteem.

Me and My Shadow

I watched my shadow
As it moved along with me,
It mimicked all my motions
As far as I could see.
So you call me foolish
For watching this movement on the wall.
But as long as I am present,
My shadow is standing tall.
We're constant companions,
My shadow and me,
And if you do not have one,
My friend, you're up a tree.
I tried to hide from mine for a moment,
By putting out the light,
But that didn't fool him,
He was just hiding from my sight.
My shadow is a faithful friend,
And sort of funny just to see.
Never asks for anything,
Just wants to be with me.
As I pondered on the problem,
And wondered what to do,
It suddenly dawned on me.
One is really two.

Men of the Sea

I'm standing on the dock
As a ship comes slowly in.
The tugs nudge her gently to her berth,
I wonder where she's been.
Has she traveled half the world around
To deliver her cargo here?
Did she encounter foul weather,
Was there any private fear?
These men that guide these ships
That sail the ocean wide
Are strong and hearty men,
And they have their private pride.
Don't be fooled, it's a lonely life
Most seamen will agree,
But it's a challenge
Extended by the sea.

Meridian Dilemma

Longitude runs north and south,
Latitude runs east and west.
They're used by travelers
To find location at it's best.
But there's a dilemma here you see,
That's given little thought.
There are places where
All of this is for naught.
Answer a question
With consideration if you may.
We know at any given longitude
It's a certain time of day.
Here is the question
To tantalize your mind.
Follow any line of time,
As it reaches north or south to find,
The time of day it is
When you reach either pole.
And here's another question,
As you reach for your goal.
What day of the week,
As well as the time?
This is my question,
Just put to rhyme.

Muted Beauty

Summer moves toward autumn,
The days are not so long.
The birds still sing in the daytime,
In the evening, the crickets chirp their song.
The flowers of the season
Begin to show their face.
Not as bright as summer,
They show a sense of nurtured grace.
Muted tones of reds, and orange, and yellows,
Deepened tones of rust and brown.
The sweet aroma of petals and seed,
Darkened green complete the crown.
The morning air has a crispness,
A hint that summer is on the wane.
Too early for the leaves to change,
But soon, just the same,
A time of reflection
The changing seasons seem to bring.
A time for remembering,
And if lucky our hearts will sing.

Memories of Franky

When I was young,
I was up at dawn.
Things to do,
No time to yawn.
Places to go,
Adventures to find.
I shared them with you.
Those were the years you defined.
We went to war
Side by side,
Did our duty,
Came home with pride.
Time has past,
We've both gone our way.
To form us a family
For a future day.
I'm in the east,
You're now in the west.
But I can't forget,
You were still the best.
I think of you often
As I reminisce,
And I hope your life
Is filled with bliss.

My Best Friend

So many words have been written
About who is man's best friend,
And with all the friends I have,
It's my dog that wins in the end.
This isn't competition, this situation,
With my family and those that I care.
It's more of a tribute to someone
That's so loyal and fair.
In good times and bad
She's right at my side,
As we walk through life together,
Both of us beaming with pride.
At night she sleeps beside the bed.
In the morning I wake with a kiss.
She's saying to me, I believe,
Lets start another day of bliss.

My Dad

I wish I had you longer,
But it wasn't to be.
You lived in a time
Before my generation and me.
You worked very hard
To put a roof overhead.
You had to struggle
To see we had bread.
Disease was rampant,
Medical knowledge short,
And, yes, you were the one
Of many that it caught.
I love the vague memories
Of days with my Dad.
They were too few,
That's what makes it so sad.
But just for a while
I was so proud.
My Dad was my hero,
He stood out in a crowd.

My Daughter Carol

To have a beautiful daughter
With an inner strength so strong.
She has her own battles,
She makes right out of wrong.
So I write a verse or two
About this girl I love.
I know she can lick the world,
And remain gentle as a dove.
Today is hard for you to smile,
But tomorrow, tomorrow the sun will shine.
When the clouds have passed us by
And all the sky turns blue,
The whole world will know
The conqueror was you.
Your fortified with so much strength,
The beauty that is so rare.
Your dad is so proud of you,
These words we must share.

My Father

My father was a mariner
Whose work was on the sea.
He traveled to far off places
That I will never see.
I wonder if he was lonely
On the treks he had to make?
But he went forth anyway,
For his families sake.
He brought home gifts
From other lands.
We children were so proud,
Because our father was so grand.
The only gift my mother wanted
Was to hold him in her arms,
Where once again as before,
She held his mighty charms.
I didn't have my father long,
He was taken very young,
But he left me a legacy
Of memories and adventures to be sung.

My Friend

I have a friend.
How do I know?
An inner feeling
Tells me so.
Someone who listens,
Someone who's there
With the right word
Whenever there's a sense of despair.
Ready to listen,
Ready to advise,
Not always the answer,
Always a word to the wise.
It might be you
As you read this rhyme,
Some don't know
Until there's a time.
And when it appears
That friend will stand out
Without ever knowing
What the problem's about.
I love you dear friend
For all that you do.
I love you dear friend
Because you are you.

My Great Grandchildren

I am the king of the Mountain,
I am a man of a dream.
You wonder what I'm saying,
You wonder what I mean.
Three beautiful daughters,
Most would think that enough.
Then comes twelve grandchildren,
Were my girls calling my bluff?
Not on your life,
They knew what would be.
Their children would grow up,
And then I'd see.
The next surprise,
I should have known.
I now have five gorgeous great grandchildren.
Again the seeds had been sown.
That's only the beginning,
I know what is to be.
There's going to be more
For this great granddad to see.
Note these names
And remember them well,
Makena, Dakota, Joshua, Colin, and Sarah.
How could a man ever foretell.

My Mother

Small of frame,
A giant of heart.
She cared for her family
From the day of its start.
My mother worked so hard each day
In a time long ago,
When family was the word
And in and out they would flow.
Basics were the only thing
Those times had to share.
Wealth was for the very few,
But my mother didn't seem to care.
The first thing in the morning
We children were the prime,
And while at school we never knew
She was working all the time.
Mothers deserve more credit
As they prioritize their day.
My mother put everything
Before herself and play,
And for her trouble long ago
She was called to leave us young,
A loss of love so dear,
My mother was an angel, her legacy unsung.

My Sister Betty

Sister and brother,
What does it mean?
The closest of kin,
No question it seems.
When children are young,
Each was just there.
Until becoming older
When they learn how to care.
By then each would have family,
And a mate of their own.
The years rolled by
And distance was sown.
Betty, my sister,
There's been too many lost years
That we should have shared joy.
But because they are missing it sometimes draws tears.
If I could roll back time,
No matter how far,
Our lives would be closer,
And you would be a star.
Time doesn't return to try again,
But knowing you care lessons the pain.
For once we both shared
The same family name.

My Sister Bunny

I had two sisters
When I was just a boy.
The older was my cousin,
And to our family she brought joy.
She had lost her mother,
Her father, a man of the sea.
So what better place than our house
For a cousin to be.
Never for a moment,
Was she anything but part
Of her family that was loving,
My sister from the start.
My older sister and my younger sister
Plus me made three.
We all loved each other,
There's no other way to be.
And when she left the family,
There remained a void that we couldn't fill.
Children grow and separate,
But no matter why or where, I love that sister still.
Years have passed, time has gone,
I've wasted all those years.
But memories of our childhood
Still bring smiles and tears.

My Sloop

I pulled my sloop from the ocean
To scrape barnacles from her underside.
To clean and restore her beauty,
But naked, she looks as I gaze with pride.
A boat belongs in the water,
Not on a cradle at rest.
But now and again, she needs attention,
And this boat will get my best.
So when she needs her share,
It's a job I do of love.
For she's always brought me home,
Sometimes with the help of the guy above.
Her bowsprit points ever forward,
At the stern a wake in her way.
When her sails are full and lines are taunt,
We face another day.
She moves through the water with grace
Now that she's scrubbed clean.
Once again there's an ocean spray,
And life again is a dream.

My Son

He's a blonde haired giant
With big blue eyes,
With a temper short
But wisdom wise.
He talks too much
And walks too fast,
But his great big smile
Leaves the girls aghast.
He's stubborn as a mule
And as independent as can be,
As gentle as a dove,
But as wild as the sea.
He's a friendly fellow
That knows what he wants,
A great big tease
Who plays and taunts.
He's the pride, you bet,
Of his Mom and Dad.
He's just about
The best to be had.
His name reflects
Of the strength to lead.
He's known as "Dale",
A man indeed.

My Wealthy Daughter

If you have the time to listen,
There's a story I'd like to tell.
Of a proud and lovely lady,
And the man with whom she chose to dwell.
She's a fine example
Of what womanhood is about.
She chose her man years ago,
And there were times she went without.
But no one worked harder
Than this guy that stole her heart.
He didn't have to try hard,
She nailed him from the start.
Better times came their way,
And faith and love grew strong.
One by one children came
And life became a song.
Wealth comes in many forms,
And theirs the better kind.
Six children raised with pride,
The mother lode of riches was their find.
The family is everything,
And they found what they always knew.
Now there are grandchildren
To add to the brew.

Nature Is Always Changing

There's one thing sure in nature,
That nothing remains the same.
Neither you or I, nor the clear blue sky,
We are all part of the game.
The sands on the beach,
Or the clouds in the sky,
The stars in the heavens
As they streak by.
We age by the moment
And a new person appears.
So does all things of nature,
In the flash of a moment, not in years.
Be who we are
And give it our best.
Old mother nature
Will take care of the rest.
Every moment we spend
Is gone so fast.
We cannot repeat it,
Nor can we make it last.
What should we do
If we think this way?
Live good every moment,
Live good every day.
But in order to do that
As we change so fast,
Is to send love to others
And be sure that it last.

Nature's Bird House

Rhododendron bush on the lawn,
Not yet in bloom, but full of song.
Home to the birds,
Protected from the winter long.
You'll bloom in your time,
And beautiful you will be.
Now a home for music,
For others to hear and see.
The warmth of spring edges closer,
There's a change in tone and sound
As the birds flown south
Return to a home, they too have found.
Slowly spring moves into place,
Flowers bloom one by one,
Nourished by the spring rain
And the warming sun.
When all is in place,
It's the rhododendrons turn to bloom,
Over the home of those little birds.
A place where natures looms.

Needless Loneliness

If you think you're lonely
And no one cares for you,
If you're feeling sorry
Here's advice on what to do.
There's someone with the solution
That can tell you otherwise.
Your greatest friend is always there,
But never listening to your demise.
Go to a mirror
And meet yourself and say,
If I want a friend and confidant
It's up to me to lead the way.
Be yourself, shy or bold,
Remember you will reap what you sow.
You're the master of your fate,
Cast a smile and a friendly glow.
Others live a lonely life of solitude,
But it doesn't have to be.
Someone has to say hello,
Why not you, you see.

Nourishment

When one thinks of nourishment,
Thoughts turn to drink and food.
But stop and think a little bit,
What makes you happy, how's your mood?
Many kinds of nourishment
We require every day,
Such as love and affection,
And a hug along the way.
So you're shy and bashful,
Not forward, much less bold.
But a smile is a try at friendliness
And you'll get it back ten fold.
It's something that costs you nothing,
But one nourished by that hug or smile,
Gets a warm and happy feeling,
And even pride and peace for a while.
You just pass on to someone,
You may or may not know,
A reason for living
And set their life aglow.

Old Glory

When America was very young,
Her flags were many types,
Until Seventeen Seventy Seven
When congress designed the "Stars and Stripes".
Some call our flag
The "Stars and Stripes",
The "Star Spangled Banner" tells the story.
Then there are others more sentimental,
They call the flag "Old Glory".
Now that's a name that can't be traced,
Or where it got it's start.
But what does it matter,
It comes straight from the heart.
This country has fought for freedom,
And lost so many souls.
To keep "Old Glory" flying
Was one of many goals.
Equality, justice, and freedom
Is what this country means,
As more and more people
Come looking for their dreams.
Not all have found their longing,
Many found distress,
But all have found a freedom
To try to make success.
"Old Glory stands waving
Proudly in the breeze
Saying opportunity is there,
It's up to you to seize.

Old Ironsides

There's a sailing ship that's history,
And she's in Boston town.
She's queen of our nation,
But doesn't wear a crown.
Proud and majestic she lies at her pier,
With stories to tell and stories to hear,
Her sails furled and decks washed clean,
Masts standing tall,
Great guns guard the beam.

A hearty crew from stem to stern
Watch over her with tender pride.
They think of their homes and wonder why
So many before them must have died
In battles at sea in a place unknown,
Doing there duty,
The price of peace being sown.

"Old Ironsides", great ship of the past,
You're an unbeaten legend that will forever be
In the hearts of Americans who love the sea.
Your sails again will fill someday,
As so often they have before,
When the U.S.S. Constitution
Was the guardian of our shore.

One of Nature's Treasures

Nestled in the woodland
Where mother nature is it all,
I'm home as I sit and listen
To what is the forest call.
Tall pines, birch, and maples,
And many more than these.
Everything is quiet,
As a gentle wind rustles leaves.
Squirrels and chipmunks
Dash to and fro.
Now and then a deer,
If your movements are very slow.
There's pheasant and partridge,
And wild turkey hiding is the green
What else would you want?
Oh yes, a sparkling rippling stream
Where trout is abundant,
And the water is so clear.
A refuge from the hectic life,
And time is in another gear
We think a little clearer,
And our thoughts seem to rearrange.
In the forest time slows down,
And perception seems to change.

One and One Are Three

I am me and only me,
You are you and only you.
I can not be you,
You can not be me.
But when we are together
We are really three.
Three you say, but only two,
How can that be so?
Life is just that simple,
You and me are we.
You've been led to understand
That one and one are two,
But if you stop and think,
In life, that's not always true.
One and one are three
If you take the time to reason,
You'll find there's no other way.
One and one may be two to some,
But you and me are we.
You see love, care, and kindness
Between two add up to three.

One Day Ending, Another Begins

An aurora settles over the heavens,
A day begins to close.
Grayness at the fringe,
Turning slowly to rose.
Soft pink clouds scattered above,
Ever brighter as they spread west,
Where the heavens have become a vibrant red
As the sun slides over the horizon, as if going to rest.
Slowly the heavens are toning down,
Though the grayness still persists.
And as the sun slips out of sight,
We stand mesmerized, no one resists.
For a long time
After the darkening sky,
We're still staring and dreaming.
No one asks why.
The day, for us, has ceased,
And we rest for the night knowing
When we arise and look to the east,
On the horizon, our sun will be glowing.
Another day of sunshine,
Or maybe some rain and overcast.
But above there is glowing sun
In our heavens, marvelous and vast.

One Plus One

The World was blessed
The other day,
When two little girls
Came to stay.
Twin daughters are double
The expectations of Mum,
But one plus one
Is a beautiful sum.
Isabelle first,
With eyes gray blue.
Then Adrien follows
To double the crew.
Now a question unanswered,
You want to know,
Adrien's eyes,
What do they show?
Another shade, to be sure,
That sparkles new.
One might call it
"Blueberry blue".
They're a joy to the family,
A pride to their Mum,
And one plus one
Is a beautiful sum.

One Proud Dad

Three proud sisters,
Families of their own.
So many years gone by,
I've watched them as they've grown.
Three proud women,
One proud dad.
We've had our happy moments,
Yes, we've had some so sad.
It's not very difficult
To roll back the years,
Three little girls with
Both laughter and tears.
They grew so fast,
Difficult for a dad to cope.
They were traveling the world of youth,
Their hearts full of hope.
One by one, they met a boy,
One by one, it was their time.
They found their love,
But they would always have mine.
Now they are mothers,
And grandmothers too.
What is the "ole dad"
Suppose to do?
Be proud, what else!

Our America

There's a never ending trail
That crosses our great land.
It's a road to adventure
From ocean to ocean, laced with sand.
There are mountains and valleys,
Plains that stretch for days.
Canyons so wide and deep
You will look with awe, amazed.
Trees of giant size, you've never seen before.
Enjoy what God has done,
There's more than you can conjure.
Roaring rivers, gentle streams,
Where fish abound and thrive,
And wildlife is abundant, far beyond your dreams.
But the greatest treasure must be felt,
In this land of wealth galore.
It's the freedom to enjoy it all
And to know there's much, much more.

Our Children

The offsprings of
A man and wife,
Give their parents
Both worry and strife.
Their age is no matter
When problems unfold,
For the answers to all
Their parents hold.
From a baby who cries
While in his crib,
To the teener with answers
Both cocky and glib,
The troubles and cares,
Misgivings, and jest
Can be brought to those
Who will put them at rest.
But for all of the worry
And all of the strife
These children of ours
Are the joy of our life.

Our Moon

High above on it's lonely perch,
Sets a bright and shining glow.
Stories are told about it,
Some grow and grow.
Around mother earth it circles
Since long before our time,
And stories still continue,
Some belong to you, others are mine.
When we were children,
We heard it was made of cheese,
And as we grew older,
We see a face, if you please.
But the Moon, as we call it,
Sends it influence down to earth,
Causing ocean tides north and south,
With little change along the equator's girth.
It influences our emotions
As inhabitants of our planet.
It causes love and odysseys,
Some soothing, some frantic.
It holds man's curiosity,
So what do we do?
We find a way to reach it,
Straight up through the blue.

Our World—Not Ours Alone

Our world is made of many worlds,
And we should try to understand.
The only way to do that
Is to visit someone else's land.
Learn about their culture
And the wonders it's produced.
Every land developed differently,
Keep an open mind and be seduced.
For although you may not understand
Most of what you see,
Their faith and beliefs
Are as strong as the one of you and me.
From Japan to Singapore,
To Tibet and Egypt too,
From Africa to the Amazon,
Even in the land of the red, white, and blue.
From far away small islands,
To the land of the midnight sun.
God looks over all of us
And all of us worship the very same one.
What God is called is unimportant.
Love the Lord and your neighbor too.
For if you are sincere,
It will all come back to you.

Our World of Wonder

Oh beautiful world
Of blue, white, and green,
There's so much of you
That goes unseen.
We each have our homeland,
Where ever that may be,
But the rest is there for wonder,
It's there to experience and see.
There are those that have the ocean,
Those that have the mountains reaching for the blue.
There are those that have woodlands
With rivers running through.
Some love the prairies,
And canyons descending deep.
Each and everyone is blessed
By the place they sow and reap.
When you settle down at evening,
Let yourself be mesmerized
By all the blessings of the world
That you have realized.

Our World

It's another quiet evening
In the family rocking chair.
Back and forth it's creaking,
It's old, it's only fair.
A time to pause, a time to think,
And as my mind goes back in years
I wonder what I've grasped.
As I think of joy, I think with tears.
The world seems to faster move,
The young aren't young for long today.
Maybe it's the years I've seen,
But soon they're grown and on their way.
The memories in this rocking chair
Are some dearest of my dreams,
For I know the world today
Really isn't what it seems.
It's as it was before,
Man can't change it much,
For It's his mother,
And it's his crutch.

Out Beyond

You think you've witnessed beauty
As you walk upon the earth,
But until you've soared beyond the clouds
And traveled thru the sky,
Until you've gazed upon the earth
From a place on high,
You've missed majestic splendor,
A panorama without compare.
Wonder all about you
As you travel thru the air.
Stately white clouds just setting there
Like massive cotton floating in air.
A brilliant blue words won't define
Holds a blazing sun way out beyond our time.
There's no beginning nor an end
Nor can there ever be.
Everything is timeless
As far as man can see.
Wonder and amazement
Become a part of those
Who surround themselves with the glory
Of this land of great repose.

Part of Nature's Wonder

Heavy clouds engulf the sky,
The sun has gone from sight.
Far away cannons roar,
The storm displays it's might.
Lightning slashes in the sky,
Way off to the west.
Drops of rain begin to fall,
Mother nature at her best.
Down comes the rain,
In torrents it seems to be.
It clears the air and makes it fresh,
It nourishes all the life we see.
When it's gone, the air is clean
And again we have blue sky.
And to warm and caress us all,
The sun shines down from high.
Exciting life engulfs us all
If only we look about.
Every part of nature is a wonder
To appreciate and never doubt.

Passing of Time

The soft shadows of time
Creep slowly over our lives,
And we know not the moments
Of wasted time passing by.
The precious presence of love
Seems lost in active minds,
Full of unimportant earthly prides
Of valor, or deeds, or self esteem.
If in driving out one's inner self
A spark of fear or uncertainty
Comes forth, a light from that spark
Will show a world of those that care.
All things pass as part of time,
All but caring and love.
These, the arts man truly
Can call his own,
Are his and his alone
And all that is his, no more.

Perspective

Perspective is personal,
You see one way,
For me it's another.
You think yea, I think nay.
The way of the world
For all of time —
Your thoughts are yours,
My thoughts are mine.
Whether an object,
Or maybe a thought,
The world has bickered,
Argued, and fought.
The secret to peace
Is in this word.
But some won't listen,
Others won't be heard,
Both could be right,
Or maybe both wrong,
It takes understanding
To make strife a song.

Point of View

When you're young and go along
With what your friends all do,
Peer pressure is what it's called,
It's not the thing for you.
But when you become older,
It's thought another way.
Now it's known as fashion,
The thing to do and say.
Think upon these words,
You judge if this is right,
But don't forget your younger days,
They're not that far from sight.
Young people are given a bad fare.
They could think alone, true,
But now who decides what you will wear,
Red, green, or blue?
Clothes are loose,
Then they're tight.
Who is to judge
If you look a sight?
White shirts, now it's pastel.
That you say is not the same.
Some would say peer pressure,
But fashion is it's name.

Pride, Joy, and Love

To you, and you, and you,
Pride, joy, and love.
A prize beyond anything
That could be expected from the Lord above.
To have three daughters grown,
To have so much pride.
All with families of their own,
But when needed, at my side.
A father trains and teaches
When his offsprings are young,
And as the girls grow older,
The father's learning has begun.
They give care and understanding,
And, yes, wisdom in return.
It's not difficult to realize
From my daughters, I can learn.

Private Problems

Is torment a part of you?
Do you suffer all alone?
No one knows your troubled moments,
As you suffer to the bone.
Our mind is a lonely place
For no one else is there.
Maybe an understanding confident,
Someone who will take the time to share.
Someone who understands you
And what your going thru.
Many times it must be
Someone that's been there too.
The mind is a place
That doesn't show it's pain,
But never the less, it's problems
Will torment while they reign.
If you know such a person,
Try to help along the way.
Believe what they tell you,
They're living a private hell almost every day.

Private Treasures

Memories are our private treasures,
A pot of gold, if you will.
All the things that went before,
Yes, there with us still.
If they are pleasant thoughts,
They give us cheer today.
There are days not so pleasant,
Here memories bring dismay.
If there is a solution
For those who would like to forget,
It's give your all to others
And not worry where your set.
The good that's done today
Is the memory for tomorrow,
And there will be days ahead,
From the past you may borrow.
Think good thoughts now,
You'll feel better if you do,
And down the road aways
The memories will come back to you.

Proud of My Grandson

Stand tall young Dale,
Walk with pride.
Throw back your shoulders,
And lengthen your stride.
No, you can't lick the world,
But you can show them your way.
Say to yourself, I can do that.
Then, go out and show them today.
Take pride in yourself,
You're special you know!
Believe in yourself and family too,
Your future depends on what you now sow.
And while you're doing all of this,
Put a big smile all across your face.
A wink of your eye won't hurt a bit,
And say to yourself, I'm leading this race.
All of a sudden, it all comes in together,
You've matured and realize,
You're bigger in knowledge,
You're larger in size.

Quest of Man

Hark to the roar above
Of power surging high,
Carried on the wings of might
In a wondrous sky.
Made by dreams
Of men with view
Of such that
Most have never knew.
What keeps you where
You are up there,
What moves you on
And thru the air?

Your just a babe
In this age of flight,
As man moves on
With far flung sight
To what lies out there
Beyond the star.
So near it seems
But yet so far.
This quest of man
To conquer space
Now moves on
At a quicker pace.

The goal we've set
Does have no end,
And all man learns

He has to rend
From what we call
The outer space.
Because out there
We have a place.
What it is
We do not know.
We only know
That we must go.

Questions

Did you ever wonder where the water goes,
When you set your boat on the sea?
Did you ever wonder where the wind is from,
When it blows on you and me?
What happens to the daylight
When evening comes around?
What happens to the green
When leaves turn red, yellow, and brown?
What happens to yesterday
When today rolls around?
How come tomorrow
Is no where to be found?
What happens to your voice
When you speak your piece?
What makes them fly in formation,
Those wonderful Canada Geese?
Where do feelings come from,
Where do they go?
What causes the twinkle in your eye,
What makes the teardrops flow?
As you ponder over all these words,
New thoughts begin to be.
The endless circle goes round and round,
All answers are not there to see.

Rainbow of Life

Competition, competition,
From the day we are born.
Who will win the rose,
Who will hold the thorn?
Life is a beautiful battle
Made of love and fear,
One leads to the other,
And that makes life so dear.
Imagine a rainbow
Of colors merging with each other,
One end is you,
The other end your brother.
If everyone imagined
Their life a rainbow part,
How well they would get along
From the very start.
Their color is a path
In this archway of grace,
Where we have the challenge
Of caring, no matter what the race.

Read On

The written word is a special picture,
Seen by all in a different way.
It tells many stories
To those that let imagination stray.
No two minds wander alike
Along the lines they read.
Each perceives the writing differently
As the words plant their seed.
A picture tells a story,
But the written word invites you in.
You find yourself in another world,
An exciting experience could begin.
Where you are and how you think;
The words will tell you this.
It might be romance or adventure,
Could be turmoil or blessed bliss.
Read on and learn of life,
Read on and chase a star.
It may take you nowhere,
It may take you, oh, so far.

Red Cloud

Just an Indian brave,
Tall, strong, and proud.
One of many thousands,
This man called Red Cloud.
Back off white man,
This is my land,
And where I am
Is where I stand.
All across this country,
His brothers spoke as he,
Only to be overcome
By numbers they could not see.
Yes, the white man
Took this land so wild,
And made it what it is today.
Civilized maybe, but surely defiled.
What is civilization
As it relates to man?
The Indians, they were civilized,
But not to the white man's plan.
Where are all the Red Clouds now?
Their voices seldom heard.
Out on reservations,
No longer free as a bird.

Relief with Violence

The heat and humidity are running high
And have for many a day.
Rain we need and rain is due
If relief is to come our way.
Sure enough, dark clouds appear
And slowly engulf the sky.
Foreboding gloom has changed the air
And soon the clouds will cry.
Across the heavens lightning streaks,
Followed by a smashing boom
Of thunder that shakes the earth,
Then disappears amidst the gloom.
Now the rain begins to fall
And where the droplets hit
The parched and dried out land,
Dust springs up a bit
And settles back to be
Drenched with welcome rain.
All the while lighting bolts
And thunder resounds again and again.
Heavier now is the downpour
As if the clouds had burst.
The rain is quick to quench
The dry land's yearning thirst.
There's a violence in the sky today,
But only for a while,
For a storm like this is transit
And when it's gone we'll smile.
Because there'll be a freshness

In the air and all about.
All will feel younger
With the urge to dance and shout.

Reminisce and Dream

The porch swing sways to and fro,
I sit alone and meditate.
The world will hurry on its way,
But I prefer this quiet state.
To reminisce and dream,
To take the time to slow.
To take my mind and settle in
To that hidden place I go.
A respite from our hurried times
May only last a while,
But it will transfer a frown
Into a charming smile.

Reminisce in Metaphor

Have I reached a point of no return?
I sit and wonder, and yes, I yearn
Of days gone by.
Sometimes bringing a tear to my eye.
I tried so hard so long ago
To capture my dream, and when I did
I kept it awhile and cherished it so.

But I didn't hold tight
To the wheel of my ship.
The winds picked up
From out on the sea,
And the rocks came quick
On the side to the lee.

If only I'd grasped the value of wealth
That I had acquired, but not by myself.
The world like the sea
Knows not of repent,
Or precious time
That was never spent.

Take with you along the way,
What you must know
And I cannot say.
Follow the wind
And shine in the sun,
Enjoy and be happy
For God's work has only begun.

Reminisce

Let your thoughts
Roll back in time
And reminisce of
Those days sublime,
When you were young
And the world seemed so
Bright that all about you
Seemed to glow.
Forget what's now
For a little while.
Let the past bring forth
In you a smile.
Nothing has changed
But point of view.
Today is the same
As the time you knew,
And years from now
When today will be then
You'll look back
To "those good ole days when".
It's time that mends wounds
And erases from thought,
In order that happiness
May overcome distraught.
Exalt this time
And abound in cheer,
For tomorrow,
Today will be yesteryear.

Restless Yearning

I yearn to have
The wind in my face,
Where the air is wet
With a salty taste.
Sails overhead,
A deck under my feet,
I yearn for the place
Where the sky and sea meet.
It's off in the distance,
Just out of reach.
Yet over the horizon,
There's another beach.
The space between me
And what's out of sight
Is my beautiful blue green sea,
And all of it's might.
What calls me off
To this restless sea,
Holding more life
Than we'll ever see?

Rhododendron

Cerise reds, pales of pink,
Adorn the view,
With shades of green
Forever showing through.
The blossoms are many,
Each six inches in size,
For all to gaze and revere
If they use their time wise.
A beautiful bush,
It's part of the joy
Of life in it's grandeur,
Given to every girl and boy.
One more grace and wonder,
Given by God, our lives to enhance.
One of an endless medley,
None put here by chance.

Riches from the Past

Yesterday I was a little boy,
Today I'm an older man.
Now I don't have a problem with that,
It's all a part of the plan.
Those years in the middle
Sometimes get a little hazy.
Did the years fly that fast,
Or did I stop to admire the daisy?
I remember most everything in time,
I just don't know where they went.
They were the days of wonder
And most were well spent.
I've decided as I write these lines,
That I produced a world of love.
Just look at my family,
My prize from up above.
Those days in the middle,
A time of life's sowing.
Today I have the memories
Of my family while growing.
Life is not all roses,
With them comes a thorn,
But all the memories scattered
Are the life that's never gone.

Riches

I have no money,
I have no gold,
But I have the riches
Of growing old.
Yes, I wonder where the years have gone,
I wonder where they went.
Have I used them properly,
How have they been spent?
The answer is my children
As I've watched them grow.
Now they have children,
The fruit of what I sow.
But that isn't all my wealth,
The rest, I would never dream.
My children's children have their children,
As I sit back and beam.
There is no greater wealth than this,
To see your family grow,
And I often wonder if
All this, my parents know.

Sails Full

A sleek lined schooner,
Sails full blown,
Heeled to the starboard,
Out to sea to roam.
What a beautiful picture,
Adventure at it's best.
It puts a spark in a sailor,
He'll face the world with zest.
The breeze is off the port side,
A spray is in the air.
Sometimes there is company,
Flying fish everywhere.
Other times it's dolphins,
Competing with delight.
Always just ahead,
Never out of sight.
The bow dips into the sea,
Then comes surging up.
Exhilaration is everywhere,
Surely the Lord has filled our cup.

Salem's Vessel—Friendship

In seventeen seventy nine
A proud ship slid into the sea.
an East Indiaman vessel,
Strong and as beautiful as she could be.
Seventeen sails adorned her,
Three great masts standing tall.
Salem was her birthplace,
She was the pride of all.
Oh, so many voyages,
Oh, so many seas,
From Europe to the Orient
And Java if you please.
But she was captured by the British,
Eighteen twelve was the year.
She served her country honorably
And so ended her career.
Now Salem has a replica
On her way to her first home
Starting the day the keel was laid,
But her mission isn't to roam.
What you see is history,
Part of what made our nation great,
And we'll stay that way only
If we remember what's at stake.

Searching

Boundaries, boundaries, they nonexist,
Only impediments in the way
Of the minds of men and women,
Searching, searching everyday
For something new that never was,
For something there, we never knew.
Conjuring in their minds
Of things we have no clue.
Boundless are the things to be,
Endless are the things we do not know.
But one by one the secrets deep,
Will reach the surface and we will now.
Our mind we use to search unknown
May itself be the greatest lure
In the everlasting quest
To reveal to us what is so obscure

Serenity

Look upon the ocean,
Gaze upon the sea.
Dream about another world
Little known to you and me.
Beneath the blue green waters,
Never seen by human eyes,
Creatures by the millions
Live, abound, and thrive.
You stand upon the shore,
Now look beneath your feet.
What you see are seashells,
But they were homes to those among the deep.
The ocean and its life
Surely is another place
Where God and his glory
Have spread eternal grace.
What ever man has gained
In the time he would be,
Would not have come about
If it wasn't for the sea.
Sometimes it is angry,
Violent beyond control.
Other times serenity
Soothing out our soul.

Shadow

I have a constant companion,
A friend without compare.
Devotion is a part of her,
A love only we shall share.
Nothing is ever asked from her
But to be at my side,
To go thru life together,
She wants to share the ride.
My dog is known as Shadow
And she is black as she can be,
But those big brown eyes
Are difficult not to see.
I guess there is something
That I really must confess.
She also loves the world
And everyone, I should guess.
Do you know many people
As you cast your thoughts around,
That can stand up to that portrayal
On any type of ground?
If you find a friend as I have,
That will share more love than she,
Then you've found yourself a treasure
Much deeper than the sea.

Katheryn

No fairy tale these lines to tell,
Coming from the loved ones around.
It's all about a little "bug",
And where this "bug" is bound.
One day it transformed itself
Into a teenage brown-eyed girl,
Who grew to be so lovely
All the boys were in a whirl.
Along comes this gallant knight,
Self-assured and strong.
This lass is mine, he thought,
If I fight off the mighty throng.
He courted and he wooed her,
And captured her young heart.
He never fooled her mom and dad,
He had their favor from the start.
Now a full grown woman—she is Katheryn,
Married and a wife.
Time to start a family,
And glorify her life.
A little girl is coming,
Yes she's on her way.
In just a little while,
She'll be here to stay.

George C. Clements

Sharing Love

What would the world be without loved ones
To bring out a smile or tear?
What would it be like to have no one,
And live alone with fear?
But just who are these loved ones,
Are they family or are they more?
Are they friends with a welcome
Each time you appear at their door?
Most of us dream of happiness,
To some it's reaching for a star.
To others it's all around them,
Always close, never far.
To receive, always remember,
You must give of yourself and share.
But whatever you do, don't construe
That there's no one out there to care.
Extend your love all around,
It will come back to you ten fold,
And the age of the one's that love you
Matters not, young or old.

Snow King

Snow is in the air
And heavy on the ground.
The noises that you hear
Are joy an splendor in sound.

No school today,
Only a hill to slide down.
A snowman in his proper place,
For now the king of town.

If your heart is of childhood,
It matters not your years.
Go and join the children
And later you'll have happy tears.

When the day is over
And the crisp air has turned your cheeks red,
You'll reminisce of your childhood
As you ready for your bed.

The next day will be brighter,
A sparkle in your eyes.
For just a little while
You were a child to your surprise.

Snow and the Pines

The wind blows out of the northeast,
Snow falls in a heavy flow.
A blanket in the making,
Gathering on everything below.
The sky above is gray,
Dark clouds, heavy with this white
That gently lands without a sound,
And leaves a wondrous sight.
Winter is for the hearty souls
That hold a zest for life.
Who appreciate its beauty
Beyond the winters wetted knife.
Down, down the falling snow,
Deepening as we watch it land.
The wind picks up its tempo,
Truly a beauty grand.
The tall green pines hold their ground,
Determined to stay green.
This is their countryside,
Here, they are the regal queen.
With snow falling at their feet,
Their majesty may be seen.

So Many Are Lost

Cannons thunder,
Bullets whine,
Young men die,
Old men dine.
The way of the world
Since people evolved.
Old men challenge,
Young men resolve
To fight for an ideal
Most don't understand,
But they believe
It's protecting their land.
Old men know better,
They've seen it before
When they were young men
Sent to fight for a score.
They've watched men die,
They know the cost.
Why don't they learn?
So many are lost.

Solace of the Sea

I'm on a boat a sailing,
A sailing on the sea.
The sails are full and beautiful
As she heels to the lee.
A wave comes a washing
Over me and the crew;
It really doesn't matter,
The sky's a brilliant blue.
The sea is rolling gently,
The world is big and bright.
All my cares and problems
Are fading out of sight.
There never was a freedom
Inside a person's soul,
That could give greater comfort
Than a good boat's gentle roll.
There's a seagull on the spreader,
His respite from the sea.
He'll stay aboard awhile,
Then away, for he is free.
As we sail on we must remember
That we're a guest out here.
The sea is the ruler,
There is nothing to fear.
Pay homage to this expanse
Of water we call the sea,
She will watch over us
If we obey the rules that be.

Something Very Special

A daughter grows to motherhood
As her mom and dad look on.
Every day is a revelation,
Every moment is a song.
That little girl so playful,
Reaching out for your hand,
Is fast growing to adolescence
Where very few of us understand.
You feeling that your losing her.
You're wrong in this worry
For you're really becoming near.
As your thoughts and ideas mingle
You see many things the same,
And from that close dawning
You both will really gain.
An understanding parent
Must learn to realize
That an understanding daughter
Has grown and is also wise.
Maybe now she is a mother,
Could be the time has not arrived,
But when it does, you'll look back
And noticed you've both survived.

Special Touch

My love compels a burst of words
As thoughts flow through my mind.
My soul's ablaze and your the flame,
To all but you, I'm blind.
A harvest moon at evening
Casts its mystic spell,
But I really never noticed
Until on you it fell.
The sun comes up each morning,
The sky is red and blue,
But brilliant as it may be,
It can't compare with you.
Trees stand tall, flowers grow,
And gentle meadows sway.
In the midst, a gentle brook
Goes winding on it's way.
God touched the earth
And gave beauty form,
And as he did, a special touch.
He sent you to adorn.

Spring

This time of year
That is known as spring
Brings back the robin
And his song to sing.
The buds are out
And the lilacs bloom,
And not far behind
The roses loom.
The sky is bright,
Then full of rain.
The earth is drenched.
The sun again
To warm the earth
And those thereon
Comes surging thru
Like another dawn.
The grass turns green,
The air is clear,
And in the midst
Love does appear
To spread it's yoke
On boy and girl,
And make their hearts
Begin to whirl.
Oh, spring you are
The birth once more

Of all in life
That came before.
So cast your spell
And let it fall
Upon the shadows
Of us all.

Square Dance

My friend, can you dance
To the fiddler's call?
Have you ever been down
To a square dance hall?
The folks that you meet
As the people arrive
Are the finest of people
This world can derive.
And as we wait
For the fun to begin,
A spirit of fellowship
We can feel filter in.
Then all at once,
There's music in the air,
And the caller sings
"Lets form your square"
Eight nice people,
Ladies with a gent,
Four handsome couples,
All enjoyment bent.
Now take just a moment,
To look about the hall,
A host of squares
Just waiting for the call.
An "allemand left"
Or a "do-si-do".
The dance has started,
Look at them go.
Eight to the center

And give with a yell.
What better way
Your cares to dispel?
The bright lively colors
In the ties and shirts
Are only excelled
By the dresses and skirts.
And when the dance is over
And all are tired to the core,
Everyone will clamor
To "give us just one more".
But before we leave
And call it a day,
Let's thank the one
That helped make it so gay.
For a shake of the hand
And a pleasant smile
Will make the caller's job
Well worthwhile.

Sturdy Stuff

The sea is raging madly,
The helmsman holds the wheel tight.
The ship pitches back and forth,
The gunnels out of sight.
She rights herself,
The scuppers drain,
The rigging bare of sails,
Except the tiny storm sail taking all the strain.
The bow dips in the trough,
Then explodes thru the swell.
Mighty is this ocean,
Few know it well.
The vessel creaks and moans,
It's saying I've had enough.
This crew and vessel
Are made of sturdy stuff.
The storm won't last forever
And when the voyage is run,
We'll take our beloved ship
And rest her and us in the sun.

Success

There are two forms of drive
That push men to success,
And one is the better
We all must confess.
First comes the man
That because of some strife,
Thinks that he always
Must battle this life.
The other's a man
That's the heart of this nation,
For his force is derived
From a loves inspiration.
You are only as big
As the heart you encase,
And you are only as strong
As your soul's embrace.
So wherever you go,
And whatever you do,
Be sure to spread love
As it was given to you.

Sunshine Makes Me Happy

I wake up in the morning,
The sun is rising too.
Soon it will be high,
Shine down on me and you.
It spreads its warmth and light
And helps me feel good.
Every day is the first day,
I try to treat it as I should.
Yesterday is a memory,
Tomorrow is a dream.
Today is what there is,
Nothing else, it would seem.
Sunshine makes me happy,
It does the same for you.
The air is clear and fresh,
The sky's a brilliant blue.
If you find the sky is cloudy,
There's something you should know.
The sun is really shining
Straight up a mile or so.

Sweet Caress

To touch, to hold,
To sweet caress.
To love and be loved,
Then we are blessed.
To hold a hand,
To share that time.
To give to one
And receive in kind.
To share the joy,
To share the grief,
To offer to others
A bit of relief.
A gentle hug
With arms around,
To past the word
And not make a sound.
This is a treasure
Neither silver nor gold.
This is a treasure
To share young or old.
Spread your love,
It will return to you
As peace an contentment
To last your life thru.

Take Heed

America, our country,
How lucky can we be?
A land that's graced with freedom
From shining sea to shining sea.
They gave their strength and courage,
Our ancestors that came before.
So many gave their very lives,
Who could ask for more?
From the men that carried muskets
While working with their plow,
To the giants of our history books
Who led to what we have now.
How many wars have come and gone,
How many gave their all?
Freedom is a fragile thing,
So please heed the call.
Don't take our freedom lightly,
Read the books of what's gone before,
For unless we begin to learn
It tells of what we have in store.

Talking To Flowers

Do you know anyone
Who takes the time to talk to flowers?
They talk about the sunshine,
They talk about the showers.
You say you think that's silly,
Flowers know not what you say.
Listen to my story,
For I do it every day.
A little talk,
A little care,
Become a part of nature,
Interaction if you dare.
Flowers are living things,
And what do you know of them?
A pretty blossom
Standing on a stem.
Try it for a while,
And watch your flowers grow.
What you reap at harvest
Depends on what you sow.

Tall Ships

There's a windblown "Tall Ship".
Her sails are full and lines are tight.
She's a credit to her nation,
A true ambassador and a sight.
What makes a ship a "Tall Ship",
Is it the height of her masts?
Or could it be another thing
Like the history of her past.
Whatever the reason,
She's a craft of legendary beauty,
With a history of heavy sailing
And a sailor's life hard duty.
A "Tall Ship" need not
Be a ship of war.
Perhaps she was a merchantman,
And half the world she saw.
To be sure, she's weathered many a storm
And had her share of gale,
But she's a stout ship
And carries many a sail.

Tantalizing Questions

Prehistoric creatures, some think live today,
Where they are we do not know,
But many claim their sighting,
Yet no one can really show
That what their eyes beheld
Is really what they saw,
Or if imagination overcame
And their minds began to yaw.
Whether real or not,
It's a challenge to our mind,
To seek out the unknown
And see what we can find.
Even if we never know
Whether real or fascination of mind and sight,
It tantalizes the imagination,
And there are those that believe they're right.
Our world is filled with questions,
And that's as it should be,
So we'll keep on with our inquiring,
Be it the wilderness or the sea.

The Secret Ingredient

A man had a dream
Many years ago.
He wasn't careful,
His dreams didn't turn out so.
But he still has his family,
Children to be proud,
His children still love him,
So he stands out in a crowd.
All the world makes errors,
The lucky ones hold love,
And his prize still his,
They came from above.
The world isn't flat,
Most say it's round.
But this man's world is his family,
And for him they surround.
He couldn't escape
The love that flows
Back and forth,
And as it does, grows and grows.
People with these riches never walk alone,
For they have the love of family and friends,
The secret ingredient
On which life depends.

The Agawam Diner

Down on the highway
A half mile or so,
There's a diner named for Indians
Almost sixty years ago.
It's not a place of glamour,
But the food's the very best.
You're treated like family,
Not just another guest.
Almost anywhere you go
For many many miles,
Everyone knows of the Agawam,
And it always brings out smiles.
No one writes your order
As you mention what sounds good.
Everything comes perfect
Just as you hoped it would.
If you listen very carefully
As you sit and enjoy your meal,
You notice the warm and cordial atmosphere
That everyone seems to feel.

The Balance of Life

There are days when all seems wrong,
When everything seems askew.
You begin to wonder,
What if anything did I do?
You struggle on and fight the beast,
And somehow the day goes by.
You've finished work and play,
Now you settle down with a sigh.
Then to your amazement
A new dawn arrives from the east,
And everything is wonderful.
What happened to the beast?
The day is full of sunshine,
There is a briskness in your step.
The air is fresh and clean,
You're free and full of pep.
For every plus there is a minus,
And it works the other way.
For every frown there is a smile,
For every night there is a day.

The Bald Eagle

Majestic Bald Eagle
Way up in the sky,
You inspire people,
Yet they know not why.
You're our symbol of freedom,
You're independence on the wing.
You're the wild expression
That can make people sing.
It's your six to eight foot wingspan,
White head with piercing eyes.
For those that first view you,
You're a sight that draws sighs.
High in the tree tops,
You make your home.
You soar with the winds,
Way up high do you roam.
You're the essence of wildlife,
Usually gathering food.
Maybe just for you,
Maybe for your brood.
Searching for your prey with those great eyes.
And when you see it down below,
You hurtle like an arrow,
And your talons grasp it on the go.

The Beaver

The activity going on
In the busy running stream
Is the diligent effort
Of a builder's working dream.
With spirited concentration,
With zeal and zest,
He'll change the shape of things,
And give himself no rest.
With twigs and limbs,
And debris that flows,
He builds his dam
And the water gently slows.
Soon a new pond
Has covered the shore,
And life nearby
Is the same no more.
Some creatures move on
While others arrive,
But the forest, as always,
Is continually alive.
The engineer of this
Change in the land
Is the amazing beaver,
There, building by hand.

The Beginning Continues

A tremendous bang, it started,
A billion stars began to form,
And travel through the nothing
On an endless expanding spawn.
It didn't happen by itself,
This awesome beginning, we will find.
It was created by a power
Much greater than man's mind.
Oh, speckled universe of outer space,
So many mysteries, you seem to hold,
And, yes it matters what we think,
As we watch in awe as you unfold.
You're so far away,
You're just reaching us at last,
And all the time we're watching spellbound,
We're gazing at the past.
The distance, incomprehensible,
But there you shine at night,
And you have a special way
Of making things so right.
If we take the time, and give some thought,
To wonder how you began,
It was the Great Creator,
Then he added man.

The Clock on the Mantel

In my home,
Against the wall,
Among my trophies
One and all.
Upon the mantel,
A clock, my pride.
From where they ask,
I proudly confide,
It was given to me by
American Airlines with Eagle adorned.
My reward for a trust
And service performed.
Each hour the chimes
Ring clear and true,
And, yes, there are days
When I begin to feel blue.
Time stops for no one,
The clock will attest,
But as we did while at work,
Let's live with a zest.

The Defiant Dandelion

Summer has passed,
We're into autumn, some call it fall.
The leaves turned to color,
Now muted all.
The grass is still green,
But the air grows cold.
What's that out there, midst the green?
The last dandelion standing defiant and bold.
Defying the season,
You haven't got all,
One proud blossom of yellow
Warming the air, though ever so small.
This lone little dandelion
Casts a radiant glow,
Telling the world
It will stay till the snow.
Little attention this flower gets,
It's thought to be a weed,
But look closely, it's a lovely herb,
And it flowers from seed.
You've learned something new?
You didn't know?
Pay attention to nature,
And see what will show.

The First of Many

Cynthia is a woman,
But once a little girl.
Cute and nosey,
She made her parents whirl.
Until her brother and sisters,
She held the family flame.
But now the family was complete,
And her brother and sisters received a name.
Still she shared the spotlight,
She was the senior of four light beams.
A joy to her father,
An answer to her mother's dreams.
Soon, she, like a flower,
Her blossom was in bloom.
She is passing through adolescence,
Very much too soon.
Along comes this young man,
As quiet as can be,
And he stole this jewel
From her mother and me.
They marry and have their family,
Six beautiful children will arise.
Where it goes from there
Will be no surprise.

The First Step

It's said to find new horizons
One must leave the shore.
A journey starts with one step,
Just go thru the door.
But where are you heading,
Have you set yourself a course?
To wander without direction
Will lead only to remorse.
The world is full of challenge
And for those that accept,
There's knowledge, hope, and wisdom,
And a whole world to correct.
No, you can't do it all
But you can do a part.
Pick yourself a goal
And give yourself a start

The Flashing of Light, the Rumble of Drums

A flash, of lightning,
Followed by a tremendous boom.
The sky now has darkened,
Clouds covering the moon.
Another flash and then another,
More drums rolling through the sky.
The rain has started slowly,
Now torrents from up on high.
Fury sweeps above us,
Yet an awesome sight,
Mother nature restless,
She's showing off her might.
The birds have disappeared,
It's not a time to fly.
The clouds still crying heavy,
But soon the storm will pass us by.
The evening will be tranquil,
A gentle breeze will blow.
The air will be clean and fresh,
Mother nature makes it so.

The Forest

As I walked among the forest trees,
I thought of the splendor all around.
A world of solace and silence,
Yet noise from treetop to the ground.
Noise I had to listen for,
A hundred creatures talking
And beneath my feet
A crunching caused by my walking.
I breathe the air so fresh
And smell the growing green.
There's a gentle river running,
Meandering through this scene.
It's source is far away,
It's destination in my dream.
This river has it's wildlife
From frogs to striking fish.
If you're looking for tranquility
You couldn't have made a better wish.
Care for this wondrous place
If you should come and roam
Among this wild garden
That so many call their home.

The Gift of a Day

White puffy clouds
In a bright blue sky,
A blazing sun
Way up on high.
A gentle breeze,
Clean fresh air.
Trees to shade,
A day not so rare.
Morning grass
With a touch of dew.
Up on high,
A mountain top view.
From out of sight,
A rushing river passing by.
A bird in flight,
He makes a cry.
Ocean waves from far beyond sight
Come cascading in,
Then rolls back
To begin again.
Maybe some rain
To help flowers bloom.
The day has past
All too soon.

The Gift of Childhood

Once we had a childhood,
Seems so long ago.
Those days were filled with sunshine,
Our young age made it so.
Then the years bring understanding,
We learn why clouds appear.
We learn of grief and sorrow,
And what makes life so dear.
Our children deserve their childhood
And the innocence that it gives,
Where everything is fun and games,
And fantasy still lives.
Where butterflies are a wonder,
And it's fun running in the rain.
A fall and a scratch,
Why does it hurt and pain?
But it doesn't hurt for long,
Everyone gets a few.
Where a puppy is a best friend,
And all of life is new.

The Gift

We've been put here for a reason,
We may not understand.
What little part we play,
It may be small, it may be grand,
But stop and think about your life
Being grateful to the Lord above,
For giving you a chance to share
Hope and happiness with those you love.
We all influence this world of ours,
Some for good, and some for bad.
Think about your way of life,
Are you proud or are you sad?
Consider the important things,
Are these the goals you strive?
Remember help and understanding
Keeps your soul alive.
Learn what you can learn
About most anything,
Then teach you learning to others
And discover what it will bring.
We all live together
No matter where we are.
The world is small and it we share
With those both near and far.

The Heavens Are for You and Me

We just looked upon yesteryear,
As we gazed up at the daylight blue,
Out where time is endless,
Where everything is old, but new.
Evening falls, the sky turns black,
A billion stars are shining bright.
We're looking at happenings long, long ago,
Not what's happening tonight.
We look up at our sky
And wonder how far we see.
Now that depends on the star we view,
They're not as close as they seem to be.
They're, oh, so far away
We measure by the speed of light,
And every star is a different time,
They're so far from our sight.
And well beyond our view,
Untold years away,
More stars are shining,
Some new, some no longer there today.
There are those that say we're viewing heaven,
And that it may be,
God made it all
And gave it to you and me.

The House with the Creaking Door

Here's the house
With the creaking door.
I stepped inside
On a creaking floor.
Nothing but silence,
And cobwebs in sight.
But that's not the story
Of what happens at night.
Stories are told of strange events,
Like voices and moans,
And the rustle of wind
To put a chill in your bones.
The result is suspense and fright,
For no one has lived there for years,
Only low voices and sounds
That conjures up fears.
An ominous place,
Both inside and out.
No one knows why,
Or what it's about.
So for those that have heard,
It's out of bounds,
But it's just some ghosts
Making their rounds.

The Joy of Friendship

To laugh and jest,
To hope and try,
And be at rest
And chase the sky.
If you want and if you will,
Join with me
And your life I'll fill
With all the joy
That I can claim.
Just be my friend,
All I ask is you remain.
When two worlds mingle as one
And someone cares
There's twice the fun.
To laugh and jest
Through sun and rain,
And when it's done
Two friends remain.
We make our joy,
It not a gift.
Share yourself with others
And give the world a lift.

The Land and the Sea

I walk down by the shore
Where land and sea combine.
The land says that's far enough,
The sea says all of this is mine.
Yet there's a solace there
As you watch the waves roll in,
Sometimes it's push and shove,
Sometimes great battles neither side will win.
But always the serenity
From a force beyond us all.
A reminder message saying,
In our cosmos we are very small.
We live on the land,
But depend on the sea,
And their kinship together
Is what allows us to be.
The sea has it's creatures
As does the land.
Two different worlds
Divided by sand.
The peace that is felt
Down by the shore
Comes from the Lord,
All that and more.

The Legend of Lady Godiva

Almost a thousand years ago,
A date obscured by time,
A lady changed the law,
And the story is set in rhyme.
The Earl of Marcia, Leofric,
And the Lady Godiva, his wife,
Ruled over the village of Coventry,
A position he held for life.
Taxes too high, the people cry.
The lady to the Earl, what will you do?
Nothing he said, unless you ride through town
Naked, your horse and you.
A bargain she says
As she lets down her long hair.
The taxes are cut,
And through the town she rides bare.
Since modesty prevails
About Ten Fifty Three,
All curtains are drawn
So no one will see.
Now a fellow named Tom
Thought he would peek,
And for that he is blind,
No pretty sights may he seek.

The Light of Knowledge

Do you have a goal you seek?
Or maybe just a dream.
There's a big difference you know,
They're as different as they seem.
You must work for your goal,
And with that you can succeed.
A dream is different,
It's only good as feed.
A goal you work for
May start as a dream or thought,
But it's no place to rest,
You must work for what is sort.
And as you struggle with it,
Your goal will start to show.
The light of knowledge
Begins to have a glow.
And when you've worked hard and long,
Sometimes wondering how and why,
One morning, you'll arise,
Your goal, it sets on high.
The thing about those with a goal,
Is when they've hauled it in,
There's another goal ahead,
And off they go again.

The Lighthouse

Be alert, great vessels of the sea
If you should ever catch sight of me.
I am your friend and mean you no harm,
'Tis the waters around me that break up the calm.

Rocks, shoals, and sandbars
Are the footing where I stand.
You are made for sailing
And not disaster on the land.
I stand tall and proud of the duty that I do.
In mighty storms and weather serene,
I've guided many a ship and her crew.

So send me a salute as you pass me by,
For I am a sentinel of where trouble lies.

The Majestic Sea

I walk down by the shore,
Along the sandy beach.
Score on score of seagulls,
Always out of reach.
The sea, rolling gently,
The air, fresh but calm.
The gulls would take flight
If I should cause alarm.
So I sit, I think unnoticed
Absorbing this tranquil place,
Where the world is restful,
And there is no harried race.
Contentment taking over,
My mind begins to slow.
The sea can change perspective,
And contentment begins to grow.

The Mountains Gift

To see a place
And then to go,
Because it beckons
To those below.
Who will accept
It's call to come
And share it's grandeur,
Then return with some?

"Bigfoot" said lets do it,
"Can Do" was eager too.
Up stepped "Mountain Man"
To complete the hearty crew.
Step by step
Thru a land serene,
We traveled slowly upward
In a wondrous world of green.
The tranquil brooks
And rivers there,
So fresh and clear
And then, the air.
We feel very special
As the summit comes in view.

Standing tall and new.
The world is spread before us,
The mountain's gift to all
Who travel in this wonderland
Because they heard a call.

No easy journey,
There's aches and pain.
We never felt so wonderful
As we stake our private claim.
Weary three,
But on a high,
Our world is so beautiful
And as endless as the sky.

The Oak and Me

Standing tall, proud, and strong,
And I know it doesn't resemble me,
But there are times when I think
I'm kin to that great oak tree.
Look around this giant,
Spread over his domain.
Now gaze upon the land below.
Descendants everywhere remain.
The acorn is the new beginning,
The squirrel doesn't gather all.
That little acorn laying on the ground,
Will grow proud and tall.
Some already started from years gone by,
Doing their best just to survive.
Others in the process,
A family that's alive.
Now look at me, I'm a giant oak,
My descendants spread around.
Some standing tall,
Some fighting for their piece of ground.
I dare not count my heirs,
The numbers change faster than I can conceive.
But they are my legacy,
In them, the future I believe.

The Ocean—A Magic Carpet

The ocean is like a magic carpet,
It's moving all the time.
Currents in all directions,
Part of the ocean's rhyme.
Governed by the sun and moon,
And rotation of our sphere,
It seems to have a rhythm
That moves it there and here.
Warm currents at the equator
Move on towards the cold,
They travel certain patterns,
And have since days of old.
Some currents reach a point
And dive into the deep,
Then reverse direction well below,
Why and how, their secrets keep.
The ocean floor is dark and obscure,
Mountains, valleys, and volcanoes,
A place of intrigue and lure.
There's more below the surface,
Things of which we do not know,
And that's the reason
Man will continue to go.

The Ole Man on the Beach

The ole man retired,
But he can't sit still.
It's not in his nature,
Nor ever it will.
Thinking it out,
What should he do?
There's lots of work,
He can find some too.
When you're older,
There's a limit you reach.
Whether you like it or not,
You're a sailor on the beach.
So you kick up the sand
And head for the docks.
Stay away from that chair
In the corner, it rocks.
More advice from the ole man,
Keep a smile on your face.
Make someone happy, beginning with you,
And you'll do your share to enhance every race.

The Ole Seaman

The ole sea captain
Hobbled down the long pier,
Found the piling where
He had set many a year.
Thoughts go back to when he was young,
And when back from the sea,
They "Splice the Mainbrace", captain and crew.
How the years fly by, windward to lee.
Sometimes a smile,
Sometimes some tears,
As the "ole salt"
Thought back on those years.
He still wore his cap,
Now tattered and worn.
But slower his gait,
Shoulders though broad, rounded burden borne.
He takes out his pipe
And starts it glowing.
How long has he had it,
No way of knowing.
Pondering where the years had gone,
Now here he set,
Lonesome seaman of days gone by,
On the edge of the sea he would never forget.

The Path of Life

I like to think
I know the way,
Along the path,
Through the day.
I like to think
Our paths will unite,
And combine as one,
To our delight.
But you must be you,
And I must be me.
There's no other way
Life can be.
Love me for me,
Or pass me by,
And I in turn
Will help you fly.
Sweet mystery of life,
So little we know.
But it's ours to live,
And we reap what we sow.

The Pegleg Pirate

Once there was a pirate
With just one leg,
But he walked the deck
With a sturdy peg.
For he was a man
As tough as nails,
Who skippered his craft,
And could handle the sails.
He had a crew
As mean as he,
And they took his orders
And let it be.
Pity the ship
That passed his way,
For it would be his
By the end of the day.
He loved to tell tales
Back in the pub,
Where the rum flowed freely,
And tough elbows rub.
But he met his match
One day at sea,
And now he lies
Where Davy Jones' Locker be.

The Red, White, and Blue

I'm known as the Star Spangled Banner,
The emblem of our land.
Many men and women have fought and died
So you and I may proudly stand.
Don't take me for granted
Because I wave so free,
For your father and mother
Gave liberty to you and me.
When we chance to pass each other by,
Put your hand upon your heart
And count your blessings,
Most people never have that start.
Some call me "Old Glory",
A fondness from days of old,
When people treasured liberty
Much more than silver and gold.
I'll be marching down the street
One day not so far away,
And if you love your country,
You'll have a tear that goes astray.
You may have mixed emotions,
But one thing will ring true.
You are free to be yourself,
Thanks to " The Red, White, and Blue"

The Right To Judge

The next time you condemn
For a deed that's been done,
Be very careful,
Next time you might be the one.
Many deeds are tragic,
Many deeds are kind.
You see only the surface,
You cannot read a mind.
Payment is made as time goes by,
Whether bad or good is at the end.
Only God has the right
To condemn or defend.

The Saga of a Stolen Wedding

A sunlit day for a wedding,
The union of a maid and her knight.
The service had hardly begun
When two little elves came into sight.
Now, these two little gems were just perfect,
No one saw the extent of their part.
But destiny works in strange ways,
And this time right from the start.
A lovely little lass
With blonde hair cut to bangs,
And a confident lad with a smile,
Yet on them, the wedding hangs.
A flower girl in her gown,
A tux for the ring bearing boy.
They played their part to perfection,
Maybe a deviation or so for joy.
But they were so cute
In their spirited way,
Some say they stole
The scene for the day.

The Sail for Me

Two types of vessels
Plying the sea.
The ship with the engine for some,
The ship with the sail for me.
The serenity of the wind
As it fills the mighty sail,
The feeling of contentment
Whether the sea is calm or gale.
The feeling of belonging,
As sailor and ship respond to the wind.
Lines are adjusted,
Sails are trimmed.
Listen to the sounds
Of vessel and sea.
They're saying to the seaman,
You're where you ought to be.
There may be whitecaps,
Or a rolling calm
Where the breeze has subsided
And the sea shows her charm.
But no matter what the weather,
Or the sky is blue or gray,
To a sailor on the water,
It's a beautiful day.

The Sea

I sailed my ship
Out towards the sea,
Headed her out
Where the whitecaps be.
The sails were full,
The wind was fresh.
My heart was light
With abounding zest.
I was the man
I was meant to be,
Accepting the sea
As she did me.
I command my craft,
But make no mistake,
That salty brine
Has the final shake.
The sea is a friend
To those that know
That she is also
An unforgiving foe.
I enjoy the lonely
World of the sea,
For it's a place to go
To get to know me.

The Tin Goose

There was an aircraft long ago
That claims to be
The great grandfather
Of all the aircraft that we see.
The first made of metal,
The first with comfort ride,
The first with three engines,
And people flew with security and pride.
It didn't have jet engines,
It didn't have great speed,
But by it's very presence
Soon took the lead.
Known as the "Ford Trimotor",
It wasn't there to last,
But by it's very presence,
The age of passenger flight was cast.
It was fondly "The Tin Goose" named,
And part of history ,
She has remained.

The Trireme

There have been many boats and vessels
That navigate the sea,
Many innovations in design
Of what a ship should be.
Very few were sailing ships
And missile all in one.
Listen to a story of long ago,
Of an ancient Galley, fighting without a gun.
About three hundred B.C.E. the Athenians,
A power of the Aegean Sea,
Had an innovation of it's own.
A lethal one it be.
Known as the Trireme,
A scourge of the sea.
Powered by sail
Until a battle be,
Then quite different,
One hundred seventy oarsmen to the task.
Heading for the enemy,
It's bowsprit low with tip of cast.
Full speed ahead,
Rammed the enemy many a blow.
Holed many times,
The deep six for the bewildered foe.

The Unknown Brine

I yearn for the ocean,
The ever moving sea.
The beginning of all life
That we know to be.
The enormity of water,
And its ever changing way.
Where creatures live unlimited,
And the wind kicks up a spray.
The solitude it offers,
A place to clear your mind.
Whether tranquility or adventure,
It's there for you to find.
The other side of the ocean
That few are privileged to view,
Has its world down deep
Where the color turns black from blue.
It's difficult to imagine
What's at the bottom of the sea.
We know there are mountains and valleys,
And there are rivers running free.
The wonders of the mighty deep,
Will be a secret for some time,
But because man must know,
We'll slowly discover the secrets of the brine.

The Urge to Know

Why do we climb mountains?
Why do we dive into the sea?
Why explore the jungle,
And delve into what use to be?
Why do we go to outer space,
And explore the world within?
The need to understand
Compels us to begin.
Our expedition of mind and matter
Is the essence of what is mankind.
This blessing is ours to use,
To wonder, search, and find.
We've only begun to realize,
As we open each door, there is more.
Every discovery that's made
Leads to a question not there before
As long as there's a door to open,
We have the insatiable urge to know.
So we keep on opening the next one,
Because it's there, we must go.

The Weathervane

Unobstructed and standing alone
At the beckon of the breeze,
Stands a weathervane of beauty,
An instrument if you please.
Weathervanes come in all shapes
Some are large and some are small.
The one that stands on this home
Is a sailboat to heed the call.
Some say" who needs one",
And maybe they are right,
But if for no other reason,
They are a beautiful sight.
Let's not get practical,
Let's not get coy.
A weathervane to those that know them
Is a comfort and a joy.

The Wheel and Me

One of nature's wonders,
A violent storm at sea.
Waves look like mountains,
Cresting over ship, crew, and me.
She's floundering and going down,
This gallant ship of many sails,
Her masts snapping off,
She's not fighting little gales.
The deck's awash, it's every man for himself,
I hold tight to the wheel, I mustn't let it be.
The binnacle and wheel tears loose from the deck,
Over the side the wheel and me.
The Captain and crew are fighting
Just as me, to survive.
I hold tight to the wheel,
It's what's keeping me alive.

Now years later this sturdy wheel
Is mounted, a trophy, on my wall.
There it is, treasured by me,
There it is admired by all.
That wheel is more than a trophy,
It's a story of the sea,
And when people want to know,
I tell of the bond between the wheel and me.

The Words of the Lord

Most of us believe in Jehovah.
True, but in many ways.
No matter your inclination,
You're given so many days.
What you do with them,
The Lord has left to you,
And the depth of your belief
Is reflected in what you do.
The secret is to believe and trust.
Your way may be different than mine,
You may believe your thinking is right,
And that, I believe is fine.
But interpretation of the words of the Lord
Can differ with those who read.
The truth of it is, like it or not,
We all have our private creed.
To say yours is correct, and another is wrong
Is not the way of God.
To understand the source of religion
Is to understand the words of the Lord.

There's a Hurricane Coming

Not long ago
Things were calm.
A storm way off,
No cause for alarm.
Far to the south,
A hurricane is blowing.
Where it would travel,
No way of knowing.
Mighty winds and rain
In a circular motion,
Cascading down
To add to the commotion.
Oh, now we can begin to see,
Yes, it is heading our way.
Oh well, it won't reach
Way up here today.
But today went by,
And so did tomorrow,
And a couple of days
Are here to our sorrow.
So we weather the storm
That came our way,
And take our punishment
For not planning that day.

Thinking

I stood before the mirror,
Naked as can be.
I asked myself, look closer,
There is more of me to see.
The real me is not in sight,
It's hidden in my frame.
My mind, my feelings,
And my passion, these are my claim.
How do I think,
How do I care,
What do I want,
What do I dare?
Every soul that walks the earth
Have these questions to face.
Take the time, I say to myself,
To face the truth, and live with grace.
With my mind, I try to understand
And use to my best.
My feelings reflect from this,
My passion propels the rest.
I see things of which I've never dreamed,
I dream of things, I'll never see.
But if I spend my life showing love,
What else can be asked of me?

This Is Heaven

White clusters amidst the blue.
Out beyond, our sun shines bright.
The earth revolves,
And now it is night.
The white clusters are still out there,
The background still is blue.
We've turned our back to the sun,
So others may have a day anew.
The heavens are aglow
In place of blue and white.
Now we view the stars,
Sparkling in the night.
While way out beyond
Our universe goes on its way,
Creating and expanding.
Here at home, we still have night and day.
Our world is one of millions,
Yet we cling to mother sun.
We're part of a solar family,
Her children on the run.
Our earth is tilted slightly on its axis
So all may share night and day.
We are all in Heaven as we speak,
Have you given thanks as you pray?

Thoughts

I write a line or two,
Of what some will call verse.
Some may think it soothing,
But to others it's just reverse.
I like to think it matters not
What other people care,
But I know deep within me
It matters how they share
The words and thoughts
That flow with each line
Making their lives brighter
As they read this gentle rhyme.
To some, words come easy
To others they seem to stray,
But to give them meaning
There's always another day.
Put your thoughts on paper
And read them another time.
Chances are they'll be clearer
They may even be sublime.
There's something to remember
As you travel life through,
Your thoughts are very special
Because your thoughts are truly you.

Time

Time is a fleeting thing,
There never seems enough.
There are those that have it easy,
And those that have it tough.
Time is short for many,
Others have more to use.
The problem with time
Is how much we abuse.
There is nothing more precious
In all our lives you see,
For without this commodity
Nothing else would be.
Use every moment
Because it won't return.
Go to the next one
With zest and a yearn.
For yearning makes us better,
And so we will thrive.
Remember desire is only a start
To how we spend our lives.

Tip Top of the Morning

There once was a little girl
With tresses blonde and curly.
Never wanted to go to bed,
Never wanted to get up early.
Her dad use to serenade her
To get her out of bed,
And yes, to this day
The song is in her head.
"Tip top of the morning",
The words rang out each day,
And with a groan and moan
She'd be up and on her way.
She is number two
Of sisters that are three.
Neither end of the rainbow,
She is the center of all you see.
As she grew more beautiful,
A sailor came along.
He had a gift of talk,
But he didn't have the song.
Now they have their family
Of which they can be proud,
And every chance her father gets,
He'll call and sing her song aloud.

To Give Is To Receive

Down the road and in the woods,
Oh, not so far away,
Flows a gentle stream
Where nature has it stray.
There's a cottage close at hand
Where a gentle couple live.
Their love is overflowing,
They want to share and give.
And in this tranquil setting
There's a story to be told.
Of these two warm country folks,
Each with a heart of gold.
They hear a tale of woe,
Two beautiful twins in need.
Just the thing to fill their hearts,
Two babies, their soul to feed.
Please come to us to stay,
We will give you love.
Suddenly, their house fills with sunshine,
On the roof, look, there lands a dove.
Kelly and Eric took these gifts
To have as their own.
They gave, but they received much more,
A love they'd never known.

To Soar in the Blue

I want to fly
Up into the blue,
And see the world
As all the birds do.
Not in a jet,
Where man is confined,
But with the wind blowing
And the air is defined.
To soar on wings
That my mind has conceived,
And follow the currents,
My spirit relieved.
To glide thru the clouds
And emerge back in our world of grace.
I want to dive for the thrill.
I want the wind in my face.
To see all the world's beauty
As it's seen from the sky.
To do all of this
A person must fly.
I want my hair
To blow in the breeze.
I want my heart
To know all of these.

Tolerance and Understanding

I cannot be a prisoner
In a world that can't show care,
But what to do, I know not,
We must find ways to share.
Surely we know we're all different
In race, beliefs, and dreams,
So tolerance and understanding
Is the only hope it seems.
Tolerance is easy,
Try it, if even for a day.
Then give a chance to understanding,
An open mind will show the way.
And when these are mastered
Take the held out hand.
It belongs to a sister or brother,
It's there for help, not demand.
Sometimes you'll see arrogance,
Maybe even hatred too.
But these poor souls
Are no different than either me or you.
Care for those about you,
It won't take any time.
It will be your part of making
The world a little more sublime.

Too Far

The nature of mankind
Seems never to know,
That in their exploring,
How far they should go.
With other worlds
Way out in space,
And other worlds so minute,
We've yet to face.
We experiment with fate,
But we go too far
When we develop a clone,
What ever they are.
What are they thinking,
In their wild race,
To make our world
Into another place.
Life is sufficient
In the varieties that exist.
Yet scientists in their wisdom,
Continue to persist
To work towards monsters
They don't understand.
Doesn't any remember "The Bomb"
And what it did to man and the land.

Treasured Ones

Today, I let my sailboat go.
Please don't ask me why.
As we parted company,
A tear formed in my eye.
Sailing is a passion
To a lover of the sea.
Any true sailor will tell you,
"That boat is a part of me."
Everything that we hold dear,
Someday we must let go.
It's the price for our living,
We know it will be so.
Fair winds and stormy seas,
They both endear true love.
Hold close to your treasured ones,
They were given from above.
But unlike my sailboat,
They, you cannot replace.
Family and friends
Is your share of God's grace.

Trophies

The greatest of trophies
Are not found on a shelf.
The greatest of trophies
Are a part of ourself.
The siblings we spawn
Are the honors conceived,
And what they become
Are the honors achieved.
We are a symbol for guidance,
A stanchion we do stand.
A beacon for direction,
A guide without demand.
We design our own trophies
As they grow in size,
And if done with care,
Our dreams we realize.

Tsunami

The earth erupts beneath the sea,
A convulsion in the deep.
And up, up the pressure roars.
The surface, a destination to keep.
The sea begins to swell,
A giant wave begins to roam,
And thunders on to be
A giant of cascading foam.
Turning blue green to white.
On it comes like a monster of the deep,
Growing in size, growing in might.
Where will it stop, where will it end?
All in the path of this mighty surge
Is lost in it's way, over what it will descend?
Will it be land standing firm
Where begins a tremendous fight.
The land says stop, travel no more,
So forces of nature compete as might.
Soon the battle is over,
The sea will settle down
And return to it's world unknown
Below the surface
Where life was sown.

Two Ends to a Theory

Here's a theory to ponder on
As you wonder who you are.
Suppose our sun is an atom,
In a greater form of life afar.
Suppose this universe of ours
Is a minor part of so much more.
This theory can go on and on,
We haven't even touched what's in store.
Now, how big does this make us,
If this thought is the rule?
It take's us down a bit,
Even makes us minuscule.
Now before you feel inferior,
Think another thought.
For all we know our atom
Is the star of another lot,
A part of the universe
Unseen by you and me,
Something so small to us,
That we can't imagine it to be.
Before you make a judgement
Of the sanity of what you read,
Understand we may be just a connection,
To this, would you concede?

Two Faces of the Sea

Today the sea is raging mad,
Waves that reach for the sky.
The troughs between break up the green,
The wind seems to howl and cry.
Sails furled and reefed,
Storm jib a helping hand.
The sea is making known
Who out here is in command.
The rain pours down and whips my face
From the dark gray high above.
Mother nature seems rampant,
Not a day of a sailor's love.
A test for man and craft,
Fighting side by side.
Holding tight the wheel
While running out the ride.

The sea is not always thus,
Yes, it can be serene.
Maybe this is what draws a sailor back
To a world many have never seen.
To see a whale surface
And watch the dolphins play.
To watch flying fish by the hundreds,
And catch the ocean spray.

Two Men in a Dory

The sun comes peeking over the horizon.
Two old men on the shore.
They're going fishing,
Wonder what's in store.
Two old men and their dory
At home out on the brine.
These old salts find contentment
Just by casting in their line.
The old double ender
Is as old as her crew.
Many, many stories,
Some are tall, some are true.
The lapping of the sea continues,
As they remember years gone by.
As the dory rolls about
You might catch a tear in their eye.
They're remembering adventures
When they were young and strong,
Today those adventures
Are reminisced in a song.
There may be a catch or two,
The gulls are soaring by.
It really doesn't matter,
For tomorrow they'll give another try.

U. S. S. Constitution

Thirty-three battles fought,
Thirty-three battles won.
She came through, tried and tested,
She won out under the gun.
She sets today at her berth,
At rest after two hundred years,
But she's still afloat and commissioned
Long after the days of her peers.
Old Glory flies over this vessel,
And every man aboard is proud
To say, I served on the great lady,
With her flag never unbowed.
Today, a national treasure,
Who once defended this land.
If you're fortunate enough to walk her decks,
Remember the men that made her so grand.
She won all her battles, so be it,
But, what of the crews that never came back?
They gave her the glory and legend,
And of them we must never lose track.
"Old Ironsides", you're handsome and sturdy,
But you were only as good as your crew.
Americans pay homage to this warship,
And you pay homage to who saw her through.

Understanding

Judge no more
The one you see.
For what the reason,
It could be thee.
So much there is
We do not know
Of our fellow man or woman,
And what provokes their actions so.
Pressures of a harried world,
Beyond the cope of some.
So much there is to debilitate,
It governs what we become.
To override common sense
And understand what we cannot see,
Demands compassion and much thought,
It isn't easy for the mind to run free.
No waiting for someone else
To understand such complexity,
It must begin
Within the heart and soul of you and me.
Smile and reach out
With your heart and hand,
And if you do and no response,
Remember good will takes time to understand.

Verse

There are those who like to read
A verse in any form.
There are those that care little,
But for writing in the norm.
But to sit and write a verse,
Of what life is to one's self,
Is to release feelings
And get them off the shelf.
Not so much one's problems,
Nor even to express joy.
It's just a case of letting go emotions
To everyone, girl or boy.
A pleasant way of communication
About something or someone,
An expression meaningful,
It's letting shine the sun.

Waiting for Princess Emily

We're waiting for a little girl,
She seems to be late.
But we'll have the patience,
She doesn't know the date.
A very pretty little girl,
She looks just like her mother.
I've never seen this little girl,
But I sure know her brother.
Oh, I forgot to tell you,
Why we have to wait,
She hasn't been born yet,
Guess she's a little late.
But when she decides
It's time to greet us all,
Everyone will hear her,
When she makes her first call.
Mom is hanging in there,
Dad's having a fit.
But he might as well be patient,
Stop pacing and sit.
For when the Princess
Greets the Queen,
The world again
Will be serene.

Warm Summer Nights

We may travel around the world,
And see exotic sights,
But there is nothing like
Being home on warm summer nights.
For every land's attraction
That we travel far to see,
This home of ours is the blessing
Of all there is to be.
There's a wanderlust in most of us
To see what we have not.
Travel far away we go,
We're not sure of what is sought.
Yes, there's adventure,
And even knowledge we can obtain,
By seeing our earth's wonders,
Yet at home, our hearts remain.
There are those who need not wander,
Are content to stay at home.
And read of places and adventure
From the tropics to the streets of Paree and Rome.
For me, I want to see
What's far beyond my sight,
But not for one moment
Do I lose sight of home on warm summer nights.

What Do You Hear?

Stand back and listen to the thunder,
It's rumble and resounding crash.
Watch the streaks of lightning,
And it's awesome flash.
God is telling you and me
To wake and smell the flowers.
The rain comes down in torrents,
Then eases off to showers.
The air is cleansed, a sweetness to its taste.
The sun comes out, there's a gentle breeze.
Each and everything that happens,
Has the word of God in these.
Don't wait for him to talk to you,
He's communicating everyday.
It's up to you to listen
To what he has to say.
Ask the Lord for nothing,
He's given you all there is.
Thank him for his blessings,
Everything you have is his.

Where and When

Vast and lonely universe
Stretching beyond our mind,
Your extent we may never know,
It may not be ours to find.
One cataclysmic explosion,
The universe was born.
Spreading ever outward,
Stars go on and on.
Billions with their planets
Now occupy this timeless space.
Some die out and vanish,
Others take their place.
Where did it start,
This explosion from within?
Another question not answered,
When did it begin?
It started in the nowhere,
From God came energy and matter.
And He in an instant,
Caused our universe to scatter.
Some to a distance
Beyond our realm of sight.
So far we must measure
Only by the speed of light.

Where Is Happiness

I torture myself in private thought,
Deep distress tears me apart.
Lonely within and lonely without,
What do I do, where do I start?
My mind is in turmoil,
I'm straining to call.
But to call for what,
I'm not sure at all.
So few want to listen,
So few want to see.
No decision at all
Is a decision decree.
I know this can't last,
This way of life.
I must conquer my doubts
And leave behind this tormenting strife.
I don't want to hurt
Nor do any harm,
But to continue like this
Leaves me no calm.

Which Way

When we have gone
And left this place,
When we confront heaven,
We won't be challenged as to race.
What we did before,
What we do today,
Will all be recorded,
And direct us on our way.
What we do tomorrow
Might change the way we go,
And if we live with love
It will help to make it so.
We are all one large family,
The children of God.
Because someone looks different
Doesn't make either look odd.
Put your arms around
Your sister or your brother.
Show that you care for them,
Emotion going one way also goes the other.

Wild and Free

There stands Mt. Kilimanjaro
And Mt. Kenya too, a show.
And between these grand peaks
Is a land you should know.
Picture wild land,
The home of the wild beast.
A beautiful place so open
Where animals roam and feast.
Choose your kind of wild life,
You will probably find it there.
Everything from monkeys
To giraffes that stand and stare.
Zebra, gazelles, an wildebeest abound
Everywhere you go.
From lions lounging in the shade
To leopards hidden from the show.
Were talking now of Kenya,
A land with nature free,
Fighting hard to stay that way,
It's a place the world should see.
The Massai are the people
And this is their domain,
So please you curious invaders,
Let the things you see remain.

Wild Wings

It's a beautiful sight
As you look to the sky
To see a formation of geese
As they go flying by.
They fly in a pattern
Precise and correct,
Wings stretched wide
With their long gracious neck.
They follow their leader
And all keep in stride,
As they soar through the air
With grace and pride.
The Canada Geese when in flight,
Fly in the form of a vee.
A flock of birds, yes they are,
But such a beautiful to see.
As you watch these creatures,
You begin to understand,
That as well as we,
This is their land.

Winds of the Eastern Hemisphere

North, the winds from the west.
South, they blow the same.
In between it's other ways,
For each, the sailor has a name.
Starting with the, "Westerlies".
Farther south, they go the other way,
Called the "Horse Latitudes",
For reasons, a disgrace to this day.
Next, down to the equator
Where the "Doldrums" lie.
Seldom a breeze,
A baking sun in the sky.
Then coming from the south,
The "Southeast Trades" begin to blow.
After them the "Variables",
There moving to and fro.
Now the weather's cooler,
And nature's voice can be heard.
Here come the "Roaring Forties" from the west.
For the name for this region, they use the proper word.

Winter Wonderland

The time of year called autumn
Has long since passed us by.
Winter is at the door,
And the wind seems to cry.
The temperature is falling,
The clouds deepen gray.
A dampness in the air,
A storm is on the way.
The snowflakes look lovely
As they start to flutter all around.
Now the wind is howling,
The snow makes not a sound,
Falling from the clouds above,
They're coming more and more.
It seems the beginning of
A storm we have in store.
Another part of nature's beauty
When everything is covered white,
Is the awe inspiring landscape,
A wonderland of nature's might.

Wisdom

There's a time to be young,
And time for a family grown.
Then comes the elder years,
When it's time to reap what is sown.
I sit alone and wander back
To years so long ago.
I pick out memories, some sad,
But most stand out and glow.
What wisdom I acquire
Takes years to filter out.
But come it does with patience,
As I learn what it's all about.
It brings days of contentment,
Sometimes memories of strife.
And all this time,
I'm learning of what is life.
These lines could be written
By almost anyone at hand,
I'm no different than all the world,
That's the first thing to understand.

Whisper in the Wind

There's a whisper in the wind,
It's message very clear.
It says the world is full of love
And to give it to the one that's dear.
You can't hold love within yourself
And not give it away.
It surely is a part of you,
But a part that mustn't stay.
As I listen to the whisper
The wind sends to me,
Thoughts of you and all you are
Come rushing back so free.
The whisper in the wind
Is really the glow of you,
Radiating freshness,
Making everything anew.

Wonder

As I watched with awe
A bird in flight,
I thought to myself
What a wonderful sight,
This creature of God.
He's traveling on wings
And intent on his task,
With never a wonder
Or thought to ask,
Why am I here,
What purpose to serve?
What is the reason
This life I deserve?
This creature of beauty
Is for man to admire.
A reminder to him
Of goals to aspire.
The power to wonder
And the desire to probe
Can lead man
Far beyond our globe.
The bird on the wing
And the man with vision
Were both put here
By a higher decision.
So the very next time
You look up to the sky
To watch a bird
That is soaring by,

Look further beyond,
Way out in the blue
And give thanks
To what is bestowed upon you.

Wondrous Might

Surging torrents smashing over rocks and beach,
Thunderous roar that comes with each
Wave that from the ocean pushes fighting toward the shore,
Then rolls back to try once more
To engulf the land that rebukes its might,
And fends off the sea of persistent fight.
Never ending battle lasting for all of time,
Panoramic splendor and majestic beauty combine
With all this wondrous might.
Oh, what an awe-inspiring sight,
Crashing smashing from out of the deep
Where nature with her secrets keep
The mysteries of this fantastic brine
That with its waves defines the line
Of battle between land and sea
That goes on and on thru eternity.

World of Wonder

Not many take the time
Or try to understand.
Our world is a living thing,
If you will, a wonderland.
I'm down by the seashore
Watching nature perform.
It's right before my eyes,
Oh, to know what goes on.
The ocean moves to and fro,
The tide comes in, but from where,
Then leaves, where does it go?
Trees grow before our eyes.
Most never take the time
To consider what is taking place.
This world is verse and rhyme.
Our world travels around the sun
While we're at work or play.
Our world is spinning constantly,
We're given night and day.
Where did it all come from?
Take the time to muse.
Now give some thought to this,
Who put it here for us to use?

Worry Stone

I carry a worry stone,
It was given as a gift.
It's supposed to raise my spirits
And give my mind a lift.
You don't have to be superstitious
For it to console and calm.
I just remember where I got it,
And it reduces my alarm.
Good will and love is it's message,
With lots of humor put therein.
The beginning of serenity
Brings feelings from within.
Sure, I rub it now and then
To put worries in their place.
Tell you what my secret is,
I rub it just in case.

You Alone

Yes, it's enough
To know you're there.
Yes, it's enough
To know you care.
Yes, it's enough
To dream of you,
As the sun shines bright
In a sky of blue.
But the greatest part
Is what you are to me.
For you alone,
I want my world to be.
A soft spoken word
From your lips so sweet,
One tender kiss
As our lips meet.
I hold you close
And in my heart I know,
That I want you for life,
For I love you so.

Young at Heart

If you will only try
To be young at heart.
If you will only try
To give your life a new start.
It might be the easiest thing you do,
It might be the most difficult too.
The next down moment
Won't be your last low time,
The secret is that which comes between,
Those beautiful moments when life is sublime.
There's a spirit within us,
Whether burden or free.
Try to remember when you were young,
And life an adventure in all you could see.
To be young at heart is not measured in years,
What your young eyes have seen before,
Your mind keeps and remembers,
It's still ahead, it's still in store.

Your Adventure

I know not what others think,
My mind is mine alone.
Adventure is there for all to find,
It depends on what is sown.
There's adventure in the gentle life,
Watching birds and even flowers.
Adventure is enthusiasm and zest,
A spirit that gives us powers.
It can come from a breeze on you face,
Or the thrill of climbing mountains,
Or something you've considered, but never done,
Like visiting Venetian fountains.
Whatever moves your adrenaline,
And makes you feel alive
Can be your adventure,
Whether five or ninety five.
Dive deep into the ocean
To a world unknown,
Fly an open antique airplane
The way it once was known.
But the greatest adventure of them all
Isn't far away.
It's sharing with your family.
Yesterday is gone, there's only tomorrow and today.

Your Destination

What's in your heart and head
Determines where you go.
Live your life the best you can,
Work hard to make it so.
Follow your dreams if your able,
Allow no barriers to intercept.
The future is the challenge
And one you must accept.
Because it's surely coming,
As the sky has no end.
There are things that you will do
That now you can not comprehend.
You don't have all the answers
And tomorrow, will be the same,
But you'll be a little closer
As each day is a learning game.
If there is an answer
To what we call success,
It must be how we hold ourselves,
And how we self assess.

Your Share

The New Year starts at midnight,
But it's just another day.
A time of jubilation, yes,
Maybe some will change their way.
Good intentions flow like water,
Promises are made.
The world is a happy place,
But love must never fade.
It's the very essence
Of happiness and health,
We each must give a little more,
The need to share this wealth.
Smile at a stranger,
Hug a friend today.
Say something nice to someone
As you go on your way.
Don't try to suit all the world
With everything you do,
But that smile or hug
Will rub off on you.
Look for the sunshine in the morning,
And moonlight at night.
Then look at your world,
What a beautiful sight.

Yours and Mine

I want to see the Redwoods
As they reach up to the sky,
I want to see the Grand Canyon
From it's rim way up high.
Great green forests and mountains,
Rivers flowing to the sea,
Golden prairies going on and on,
They belong to you and me.
This land is filled with wonders,
Some beyond our dreams.
For every spot of grandeur,
There's something else it seems.
Slow the pace and look around,
For here the wagons rolled
To open up this new world,
And now it's ours to hold.
America the wonderland,
Not perfect but the best.
And so I have this yearning,
It could be called a quest.